Who Is This Book For?

If you've never written VBA code before this book will show you how.

This book is for Access users and developers who:

- Are comfortable with all aspects of the interactive use of Access
- Are already able to design simple relational databases
- Want to learn Access VBA skills from first principles
- Want to learn how to develop professional-grade Access applications

Use of this book as courseware

Using this book as a self-study guide is the second best way to learn Access VBA. Being guided through the sessions by a professional instructor who is also a database and Access expert is, of course, faster, more fun and more productive!

We use this book as the official courseware for The Smart Method's VBA Access course. Smart Method courses are available for all Office applications (such as Access, Excel, Word, PowerPoint and Project) and have been taken by a varied cross-section of the world's leading companies with fantastic feedback from our students.

If you would like to use this book to teach your own courses you'll be delighted to find that we also publish an Instructor Edition of this book which includes PowerPoint slides and details of The Smart Method's recommended teaching techniques.

Learn Access 2003 VBA with The Smart Method

Mike Smart

Published by:

The Smart Method Ltd
29 Harley Street
London W1G 9QR
Tel: +44 (0)845 458 3282 Fax: +44 (0)845 458 3281

Email: informationrequest@thesmartmethod.com
Web: www.thesmartmethod.com   (The Smart Method's training site)
        www.learnaccessvba.com   (this book's dedicated web site)

FIRST EDITION

International Standard Book Number (ISBN10): 0-9554599-0-7
International Standard Book Number (ISBN13): 978-0-9554599-0-0

Contents

How to Use This Book

Welcome to *Learn Access 2003 VBA With The Smart Method*. This book has been designed to enable students to master Access 2003 VBA by self-study. The book is equally useful as courseware in order to deliver courses using The *Smart Method* teaching system.

Smart Method publications are continually evolving as feedback from our courses is incorporated whenever we discover better ways of explaining and teaching information technology concepts.

Feedback

At The Smart Method we love feedback – both positive and negative. If you have any suggestions for improvements to future versions of this book or if you find content or typographical errors the author would always love to hear from you via Email to:

feedback@learnaccessvba.com

While a response cannot be guaranteed, future editions will always incorporate your feedback so that there are never any known errors at time of publication.

Downloading the sample files

Only one file is essential

In order to use this book it is only necessary to download the *Session 1* sample file from the Internet. The sample file is available from:

http://www.learnaccessvba.com

You do not have to download all of the files you will find there. The lesson and session files are provided only for disaster recovery. You'll build the entire application starting with the single *Session 1* file.

Type the above URL into your web browser and follow the full instructions available on this web page.

Session and lesson files

The best way to benefit from the course as a whole is to work through all sessions and lessons in sequence and build the sample application yourself starting with the Session 1 database that contains only data (no relationships, validations, reports, queries, forms or VBA code).

Sometimes you may need to use the book as a reference and only wish to complete a specific session or lesson. In this case you can download the relevant lesson or session file. You can also use these files if you corrupt your work-in-progress file mid-way through the course.

Problem resolution

There are a lot of incremental files available on the web—one for every lesson in this course. They have all been tested but if any problems are encountered either downloading or using the sample files please send an Email to:

feedback@learnaccessvba.com

And we'll do everything possible to quickly resolve the problem.

Typographical Conventions Used In This Guide

This guide consistently uses typographical conventions to differentiate parts of the text.

When you see this	Here's what it means
`Dim strCustomer as string`	Program code. (All code is printed using Courier New font, the same font used by the VBA Editor).
Re-makes of films are quite common, for example the classic film *Get Carter* was first made in 1971 with Michael Caine in the lead role.	Italics may sometimes be used for emphasis or distinction. They may be used for entities such as book titles, names of films and table names when such items would not be sufficiently distinct from the surrounding text without embellishment.
Select File→New from the main menu	Click on File from the main menu and then select New from the drop down menu list.
Press <Ctrl> + <Z>.	You should hold down the Ctrl key while pressing the Z key.
	When a lesson tells you to click a toolbar button the relevant button will be shown either in the page margin or within the text itself.
note You can declare variables anywhere in your code but it's good practice to do this at the beginning of the sub or function.	If you want to read through the book as quickly as possible you don't have to read notes. Notes usually expand a little on the information given in the lesson text.
important Do not click the Delete button at this point as to do so would erase the entire table.	Whenever something can easily go wrong, or when the subject text is particularly important, you will see the *Important* sidebar. You should always read Important sidebars.
tip Set up field validation, format and lookups before creating your forms	Tips add to the lesson text by showing you shortcuts or time-saving techniques relevant to the lesson.

Session1

The best way to benefit from the course as a whole is to work through all sessions and lessons in sequence and build the sample application yourself.

Sometimes you may need to use the book as a reference and only wish to complete a specific session or lesson. In this case note the file name shown in the folder icon at bottom left of each lesson page (*Session1* in the example shown) and download the relevant lesson or session file from: *www.learnaccessvba.com*.

Use of American English

Even though this is a British publication American English (rather than British English) spelling has been used throughout. This is because the Access help system and screen elements all use American English spelling making the use of British English confusing.

Examples of differences are the British English spelling: *Colour* and *Dialogue* as opposed to the American English spelling: *Color* and *Dialog*.

Putting the Smart Method to Work

Access version and service pack

This edition was written using *Microsoft Access 2003 Service Pack 2* running under the *Microsoft XP Service Pack 2* operating system. You can check your program version by selecting Help→About from the Access main menu. If you then click the *System Info…* button from the same dialog you can also confirm your operating system version.

If you are using an earlier operating system or program version this book will be equally relevant but you may notice small differences between some of the screen grabs in the book and those on your screen. There is also a small possibility that some code may not execute as described.

Sessions and lessons

The book is arranged into Sessions and Lessons. In a *Smart Method* course a Session would generally last for between half an hour and an hour and a half and would represent a continuous period of interactive instruction followed by a coffee break of ten or fifteen minutes.

When you use this book for self-instruction we'd recommend that you do the same. You'll learn better if you lock yourself away, switch off your telephone and complete the whole session without interruption. The memory process is associative and we've ensured that each lesson within each session is very closely coupled (contextually) with the others. By learning the whole session in one sitting you'll store all of that information in the same part of your memory and should find it easier to recall later.

The experience of being able to remember all of the words of a song as soon as somebody has got you "started" with the first line is an example of the memory's associative system of data storage.

We'd also highly recommend that you do take a break between sessions and spend it relaxing rather than catching up on your Emails. This gives your brain a little idle time to do some data sorting and storage!

First page of a session

1/ The first page begins with a quotation, often from an era before the age of the computer, that is particularly pertinent to the session material. As well as being fun, this helps us to remember that all of the real-world problems we solve with technology have been around for a long time.

3/ The session objectives *formally* state the precise skills that you will learn in the session.

At the end of the session you should re-visit the objectives and not progress to the next session until you can honestly agree that you have achieved them.

In a *Smart Method* course we never progress to the next session until all delegates agree that they are completely confident that they have achieved the previous session's objectives.

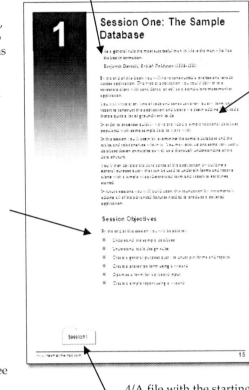

2/ In the next few paragraphs we *informally* summarise why the session is important and the benefits that you will get from completing it.

This is important because without motivation adults do not learn. For adults, learning is a means to an end and not an end in itself.

The aim of the introduction is to motivate your retention of the skills that will be taught in the following session by allowing you to preview the relevance of the material that will be presented. This may subconsciously put your brain into "must remember this" mode—assuming, of course, that the introduction convinces you that the skills will be useful to you!

4/ A file with the starting point for the session is always available for download from: *www.learnaccessvba.com*. The file name is stated here.

Every lesson is presented on two facing pages

> Pray this day, on one side of one sheet of paper, explain how the Royal Navy is prepared to meet the coming conflict.
> *Winston Churchill, Letter to the Admiralty, Sep 1, 1939*

Winston Churchill was well aware of the power of brevity. The discipline of condensing thoughts into one side of a single sheet of A4 paper resulted in efficient transfer of information.

A tenet of our teaching system is that every lesson is presented on *two* facing sheets of A4. We've had to double Churchill's rule as they didn't have to contend with screen grabs in 1939!

If we can't teach an essential concept in two pages of A4 we know that the subject matter needs to broken into two smaller lessons.

Tips, important information and notes appear in sidebars.

Each step is numbered and begins with the thing you need to do in bold type. Sometimes this is all you need to read to accomplish the task.

Step notes sometimes provide precise instructions on how to progress if the one-line description is inadequate. Notes often also include interesting information about the current task.

If you are not working through the course sequentially, a file is available on our web site that contains the starting point for every lesson. The file name you need to download is stated in the file icon at bottom left of every lesson page.

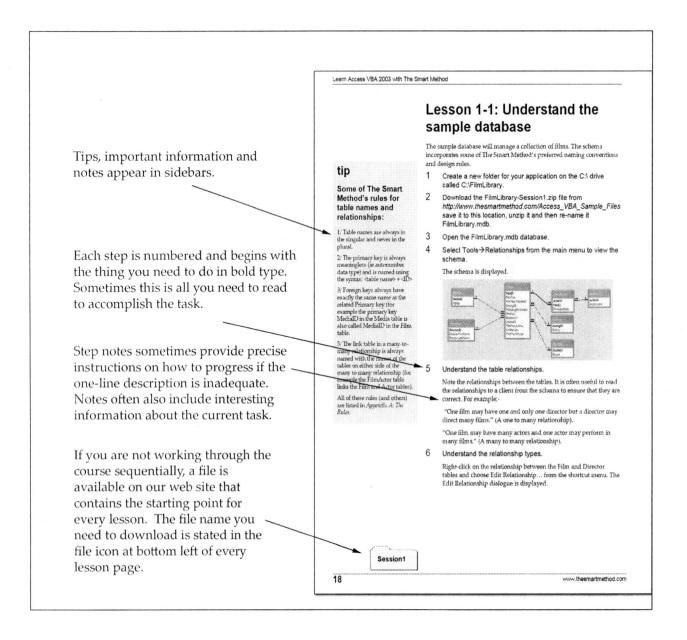

Learning by participation

Tell me, and I will forget. Show me, and I may remember. Involve me, and I will understand.

Confucius (551-479 BC)

Confucius would probably have agreed that the best way to teach IT skills is hands-on (actively) and not hands-off (passively). This is another of the principal tenets of our *Smart Method* teaching system. Research has backed up the assertion that you will learn more material, learn more quickly, and understand more of what you learn if you learn using active, rather than passive methods.

For this reason pure theory pages are kept to an absolute minimum with most theory woven into the hands-on sessions either within the text or in sidebars. This echoes our teaching method in Smart Method courses where snippets of pertinent theory are woven into the lessons themselves so that interest and attention is maintained by hands-on involvement but all necessary theory is still covered.

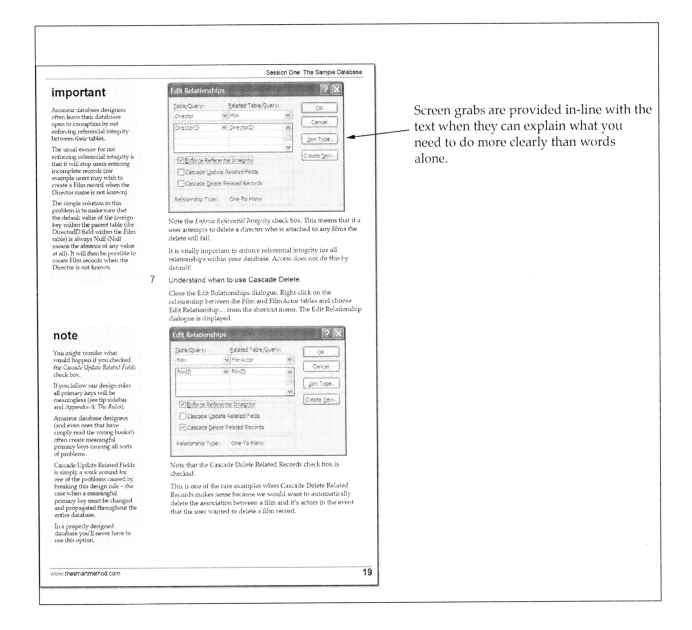

Screen grabs are provided in-line with the text when they can explain what you need to do more clearly than words alone.

Session One: The Sample Database

> As a general rule the most successful man in life is the man who has the best information.
>
> *Benjamin Disraeli, British Politician (1804-1881)*

By the end of this book you will have constructed a professional-grade Access application. The type of application you could deliver to a corporate client with confidence, or sell as a stand-alone mass-market application. The application will manage a collection of films on a variety of media such as DVD or VHS cassette.

You will write every line of code and construct every relationship, validation, query, form and report to build the application.

In order to progress quickly we've provided a set of tables populated with some sample data to work with. In this session you'll create the relationships and validations required to transform the tables into a properly constrained, high-integrity relational database.

You'll then develop the bare bones of the application by building a general purpose query that will be used to underpin forms and reports along with a simple wizard-generated form and report.

In future sessions you will build upon this foundation and incrementally add all of the advanced features needed to produce a polished application.

Session Objectives

By the end of this session you will be able to:

- Understand the sample database
- Create simple and concatenated lookup fields
- Create one-to-many table relationships
- Set default and required values
- Create a general purpose query to underpin forms and reports
- Create a prototype form using a wizard
- Optimise a form for keyboard input
- Create a simple report using a wizard

Session1

Lesson 1-1: Understand the sample database

The sample database is simply a set of tables full of data. There are no validations, relationships or default values set. Before we further develop the database you should be familiar with some of the rules that have been observed in building it.

All of these rules are re-stated in *Appendix A: The Rules.*

1 Create a new folder for your application on the C:\ drive called C:\FilmLibrary.

2 Download the Session1.zip file from *www.learnaccessvba.com,* save it to C:\FilmLibrary, unzip it and then re-name the Session1.mdb file to FilmLibrary.mdb.

3 Open the FilmLibrary.mdb database.

4 Select Tools→Relationships from the main menu to view the schema.

The schema is displayed.

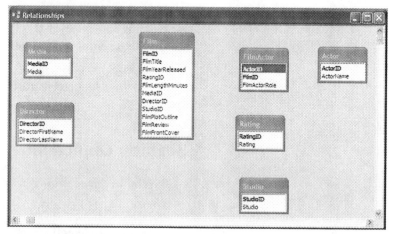

It might be a little ambitious to describe the above as a schema as we've not yet defined the relationships that will transform it into a real relational database.

5 Understand table naming rules.

Table names are always in the singular and never in the plural (for example Director rather than Directors).

You should be aware that some database designers turn this convention upside down and make all table names plural. It is preferable to enforce an "everything in the singular" convention as variable names must be identical to field names in order to conform to *the cradle to the grave naming convention* (this will be discussed later in the lesson).

6 Understand Primary key rules.

The primary key is always meaningless, has the AutoNumber data type, and is named using the syntax: <table name> + <ID>.

Session1

For example, the primary key of the *Director* table is called *DirectorID*.

7 Understand Field name rules

▓ No abbreviations. For example naming a field FilmLenMins would break this rule.

▓ If not obvious the unit of measure is incorporated into the field name (the FilmLength attribute could be measured in hours or minutes so is qualified with the postfix *Minutes* to avoid any confusion).

▓ All Field names (except foreign keys) are always prefixed by the table name. Because all table names in a database are unique you will gain the huge advantage of every field name also being unique by observing this rule.

For example, the *Title* field in the *Film* table is prefixed with the table name and named *FilmTitle*.

8 Understand Foreign Key rules.

Foreign keys always have exactly the same name as the related Primary key.

For example the primary key MediaID in the Media table relates to a foreign key that is also called MediaID in the Film table.

9 Understand the *cradle to the grave naming convention*.

The convention is as follows:

Apart from prefixes and spaces exactly the same name is used for the field name, caption on forms, report column header and code variable name.

It is difficult to over-state the importance of this convention. If you religiously observe it your database will be a delight to work with.

Access allows a caption to be defined for every field. All captions in the sample database have been named using the convention. This means that a field named *FilmYearReleased* can only have one possible caption: *Year Released*.

Lesson 1-2: Create lookup fields

If we set table relationships using a lookup field a form prototype can be generated much faster than would be the case if the relationships were manually created.

When a lookup field exists the Form Wizard will convert the relevant foreign key to a combo box with its own underlying SQL query.

Lookup fields are not a great idea for the novice developer as their delight at a quick fix rapidly turns to frustration when their application does not function as expected.

For the experienced Access developer they can be very useful in jump-starting prototype form development.

1 Open the Film table in Design View.

Select the data type drop down list for the RatingID field and select Lookup Wizard… as the Data Type.

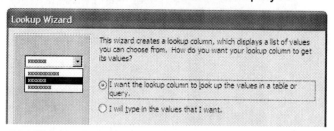

2 The Lookup Wizard's first screen is displayed:

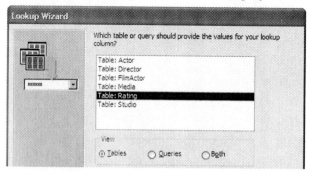

3 Choose *I want the lookup column to look up the values in a table or query* and click the Next > button.

The lookup wizard's second screen is displayed:

4 Choose the *Rating* table and click the Next > button.

5 Choose both the RatingID and the Rating Field for the lookup and then click the Next > button.

When setting a lookup field you must always include the Primary Key of the lookup table (see sidebar).

Session1

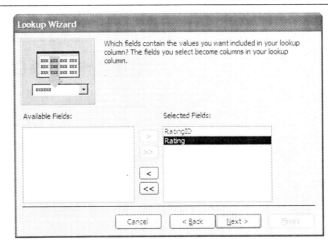

6   Sort the lookup by *Rating Ascending* and click the Next > button.

7   Re-size the lookup field if required and click the Next > button.

Drag the right-hand side of the gray box at the top of the Rating column to the right or left until you are happy with the width of the column. This will determine the width of the auto-generated combo box control that will be displayed on the form later.

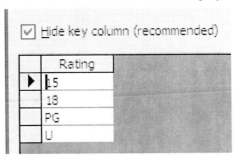

8   Leave the label at the default value of RatingID and click the Next button.

It isn't a good idea to change the name of the label here. It is better to use the Caption property of the field instead to set the correct labels for controls on wizard-generated forms.

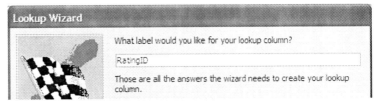

9   Use the same technique to set lookup fields for the MediaID and StudioID fields but not the DirectorID field.

Lesson 1-3: Create a concatenated lookup field

A very common problem with simple lookup fields is their inability to correctly sort and display multiple fields.

The problem

The Lookup Wizard does allow you to select more than one field but if we did this for the DirectorId foreign key the Datasheet View would appear as shown:

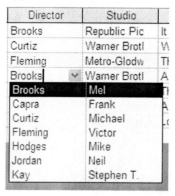

We're seeing the Director's first and last names in the drop-down list but only the last name in the Datasheet View table.

The same problem will be evident in combo box controls auto-generated by the Form Wizard:

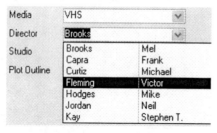

We'd like to see the director's full name, for example *Brooks, Mel* inside the combo box on the form alphabetically sorted by DirectorLastName.

1   Create a regular lookup field for the DirectorID field as you did in the last lesson but only select the DirectorID and DirectorLastName fields when prompted by the lookup wizard.

2   Switch to Datasheet view and observe how the field is working.

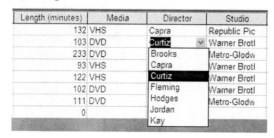

Session1a

The field isn't bad but will be a real problem if we have two directors with the same last name.

3   Return to Design View and select the *Lookup* tab at the bottom left of the screen.

Select the Row Source field and then click on the ellipsis button 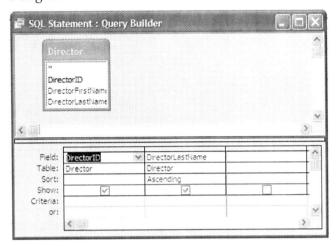 that appears on the right hand side.

The SQL query underpinning the lookup is shown in the Query Designer window.

4   Change the DirectorLastName field into a concatenation of the DirectorFirstName and DirectorLastName.

Type the following expression into the Field box to replace DirectorLastName:

```
Director: [DirectorLastName] & "," & [DirectorFirstName]
```

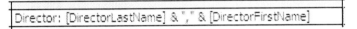

5   View the table again in Datasheet View. The lookup field works exactly as we want it to.

Lesson 1-4: Create one-to-many table relationships

1   Select Tools→Relationships from the main menu to view the schema.

The schema is displayed.

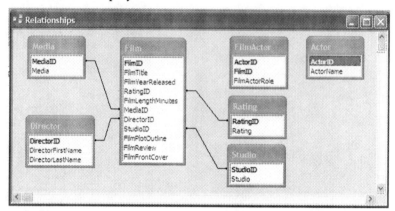

Note that the Lookup Wizard has already created *one-to-many* relationships between the Film table and the Media, Director, Rating and Studio tables. We'll also learn how to do this manually in a later lesson.

The relationship between Actor and Film is a little more complicated as it is a *many-to-many relationship*. We'll be discussing this a little later.

2   Constrain the relationships.

At the moment the relationships are un-constrained. This means that the database will quite happily allow the user to delete a director even if the record is associated with a film or films.

Rightclick on the relationship between the Director and Film table and choose *Edit Relationship…* from the short-cut menu.

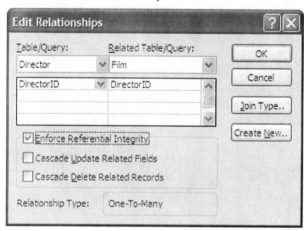

The Edit Relationship dialog is displayed.

Check the *Enforce Referential Integrity* check box.

Session1b

By clicking this box you have instructed the database to police its integrity. The database will no longer allow a user to delete a director who is attached to any films.

It is vitally important to enforce referential integrity for all relationships within your database. To assist novice users Access does not do this by default!

3   Observe the new schema.

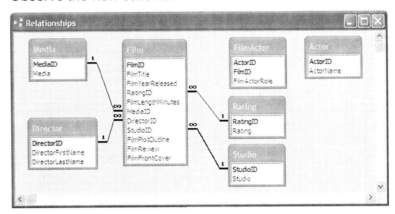

Note that the relationship lines are a little thicker and that either a *1* or an *infinity symbol* is shown at each end of the relationship.

This is how Access tells you (visually) that the relationships are correctly constrained.

4   Verify the relationships.

It is often useful to read the relationships to a client from the schema to ensure that they are correct. For example:

"One film may have one and only one director but a director may direct many films." (A one-to-many-relationship).

note

Allowing an actor to be associated with a film in multiple roles

The database enforces the following constraint:-

One actor may only have one role in a film.

This is desirable because it will prevent users from accidentally associating the same actor with a film twice.

Sometimes an actor may play multiple roles in a film and the present design does not allow this information to be stored.

If the specification demanded that it must be possible for actors to be associated with a film more than once (in different roles) there is a simple solution.

Another field would be added to the FilmActor table named FilmActorID and with a data type of AutoNumber. This field would then be included in the concatenated primary key (consisting of three fields: FilmActorID, ActorID and FilmID). With this arrangement it would be possible to associate the same actor with a film many times in different roles.

The downside of allowing the actor to be associated with a film many times in different roles is that the user may accidentally add duplicate records (ie add the same actor in the same role in the same film twice). This type of error could be eliminated by adding a form-based business rule in VBA code – something you'll learn how to do in a later session.

Lesson 1-5: Create a many-to-many table relationship

The relationship between *Actor* and *Film* is not a one-to-many relationship but a many-to-many relationship.

One film may have many actors and one actor may perform in many films.

We'd also like to know which role the actor played in each film.

The role is not an attribute of an actor, or an attribute of a film. It is an attribute of the relationship between an actor and a specific film.

In a *many-to-many* relationship the relationship is modeled by inserting a new table between the tables on either side of the many-to-many relationship. The table is always named with the names of the table on either side of the relationship (in this case *FilmActor* though *ActorFilm* would be equally correct).

The primary key of a many-to-many link table is always a concatenation of the two foreign keys from the tables on either side of the many-to-many relationship (in this case a concatenation of *ActorID* and *FilmID*).

Because the primary key must be unique, this arrangement prohibits actors from having more than one role in a given film (see sidebar).

1   Select Tools→Relationships from the main menu to view the schema.

The schema is displayed.

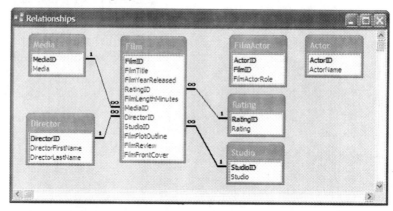

2   Drag the ActorID field from the FilmActor table and drop it onto the ActorID field in the Actor table.

It would not matter if you did this in reverse and dragged the field from the Actor table and dropped it onto the FilmActor table. Access is quite aware of which table has the field as primary key so can always work out which is the *one* side of a relationship.

The Edit Relationships dialog appears.

3   Constrain the relationship by clicking the *Enforce Referential Integrity* check box.

Session1c

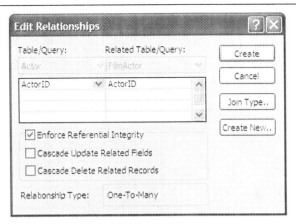

4   Use exactly the same method to create a constrained relationship between the FilmID primary key in the Film table and the FilmID foreign key in the FilmActor table.

5   Add a Cascading Delete to the relationship between the Film and FilmActor tables.

Right-click on the relationship between the Film and FilmActor tables and choose *Edit Relationship...* from the shortcut menu. The Edit Relationship dialog is displayed.

Check the *Cascade Delete Related Records* check box.

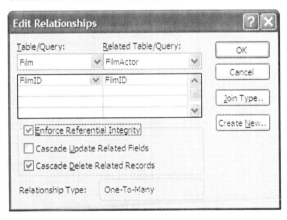

Cascade Delete Related Records informs Access to maintain referential integrity in a different way. If a Film record was deleted and related entries in the FilmActor table (defining the actor's roles in the film) existed, Access would normally prohibit the record's deletion until all related records in the FilmActor table were also deleted.

Cascade Delete Related Records will automatically delete any such records found in the FilmActor table when a film is deleted.

This is one of the rare examples when *Cascade Delete Related Records* makes sense. Normally this isn't what you want to do so think carefully before using this feature in your own designs.

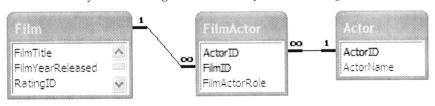

---

note

You might wonder what would happen if you checked the *Cascade Update Related Fields* check box.

If you follow our design rules all primary keys will be meaningless.

Amateur database designers (and even ones that have simply read the wrong books)! often create meaningful primary keys (such as *Telephone Number*).

Cascade Update Related Fields is simply a work around for one of the problems caused by breaking this design rule – the case when a meaningful primary key must be changed and propagated throughout the entire database.

In a properly designed database you'll never have to use this option.

Lesson 1-6: Set default and required values

There are a few problems with the current database design.

The first we need to address is the potential pitfall of users generating entirely blank records. At present this is possible for most tables.

The other problem concerns the inability to add incomplete records. Because we have created constrained relationships between the Film table and five other tables Access will not allow a Film record to be created when the Director, Rating, Studio and Media fields are unknown.

In this lesson we'll solve both problems.

1   Set a required field for the Media table.

The primary key is, of course, required and Access will always enforce this. Because we are following good design practice, however, the primary key is automatically generated, meaningless, and contains no information of any worth to the user.

It is good design practice to ensure that there is at least one (non-primary) required field in each table as this will prevent the user from accidentally creating a blank record.

Open the Media table in Design View and select the Media field. Observe the *Field Properties* dialog at the bottom left of the screen.

Set the *Required* property to *Yes*

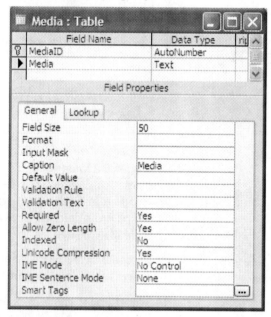

2   Set a required field for all other tables.

Set the *Required* property to *Yes* for the following table fields in the same way:

Session1d

Table	Field(s)
Director	DirectorFirstName DirectorLastName
Film	FilmTitle
Actor	ActorName
Rating	Rating
Studio	Studio

3   Change the default value to Null for all foreign keys in the Film table.

Open the Film table in Design View. Select the RatingID field and note the default value.

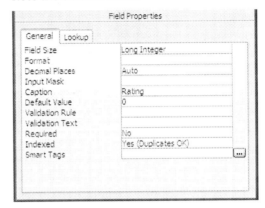

Access always automatically sets the default values of numeric fields to zero. This will cause a problem when trying to add a *Film* record for which the *Rating* is presently unknown.

Remove the zero so that the field is blank. This has re-defined the field as being of default value *Null*.

Null is an interesting concept in database systems. It indicates the lack of any value at all rather than a specific value (in this case *Nothing* rather than *zero*).

In database systems Null fields behave very differently to zero value fields. When a foreign key field has a value of Null Access will allow the record to be added to the table even if the foreign key forms part of a constrained relationship.

4   Set all other foreign key default values within the Film table to Null.

The remaining foreign key fields are: MediaID, DirectorID and StudioID.

Lesson 1-7: Create a general-purpose query

The form wizard allows a form to be created based upon a table. Thanks to the careful design of the tables, relationships, field names and captions the wizard is already able to do a creditable job of auto-generating a form based upon the film table that is capable of adding, editing and deleting films from the database.

A more flexible approach is to create a form based upon an SQL query so that non-displayed related fields are available to our VBA code. These will be useful in later sessions when filtering and sorting upon non-displayed fields. We might also wish to add calculated fields to the query result and define a sort order that is based upon a calculated field. The more sophisticated approach of creating the form based upon an SQL query provides all of these benefits.

1   Close the Table window and click the Queries object in the Database window.

2   Double-Click *Create query in Design View*. Add all tables except the FilmActor and Actor tables.

The Query Designer window opens.

We do not want to include the FilmActor and Actor tables within the query as this would result in more than one query result for each film as the Film to Actor relationship is the only many-to-many relationship in the system.

note

Right and left joins

If the joins were left at default (this is the first option in the Join Properties dialog), a join type called an inner-join or equi-join would be created. This would mean that any film record that had did not have a Director, Media, Rating and Studio record associated with it would not be shown in the query results.

We want the query to return all films even where the user has yet to enter this information.

Option 3 produces a type of join called a *Right Join*. The Right Join will display all Film records irrespective of whether the user has selected values for the foreign keys: DirectorID, MediaID, RatingID and StudioID in the Film table (ie where these fields have a Null value).

3   Drag the dividing bar down to the middle of the window and re-arrange the tables so that you can see all fields within the table and so that the relationship lines do not cross.

4   Change all joins to Right joins.

Right click on each join, select Join properties from the shortcut menu and select the third option "include ALL records from 'Film' and only those records from (the name of the joined table) where the joined fields are equal" from the resulting dialog:

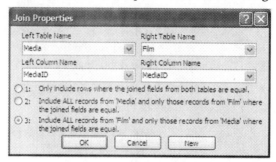

Note that each join now has an arrow at the end of the join indicating that right joins have been set (see sidebar).

Session1e

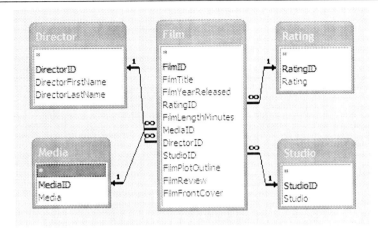

5 Add the fields into the grid

Double-click or drag the following fields into the design grid:

Table	Fields
Film	All fields (see sidebar)
Director	DirectorFirstName and DirectorLastName
Media	Media
Rating	Rating
Studio	Studio

6 Create an additional calculated field to concatenate the DirectorFirstName and DirectorLastName fields naming the new field DirectorFullName that will display like this example:

Brooks, Mel

Note that this is *in addition to* the DirectorFirstName and DirectorLastName fields in the query so do not remove the individual fields from the query.

```
DirectorFullName: [DirectorLastName] & "," & [DirectorFirstName]



                              ☑
```

7 Create a calculated field called FilmAndYear that concatenates the FilmTitle and FilmYearReleased fields into a single field that will display like this example:

Get Carter (1971)

```
FilmTitleAndYear: [FilmTitle] & " (" & [FilmYearReleased] & ")"


Ascending
                              ☑
```

8 Add an ascending sort for the new FilmTitleAndYear calculated field.

9 Test run the query and then save it as qryFilmDetails.

Lesson 1-8: Create the prototype main form using a wizard

The form wizard is a great place to start when creating a form.

It won't create a perfect form but will give you a head start. The form we create in this exercise will eventually become a professional-grade form with many advanced VBA driven features but, for now, let's see what a great job the Wizard can do in providing a starting point towards this objective.

1   Make a copy of the qryFilmDetails query called qryFilmDetailsForForm.

Right-click the qryFilmDetails query in the query window and choose Copy. Right-click again and choose Paste to copy the query. Right-click the copied query and choose Rename to rename the query.

2   Close the Query window and click the Forms object in the Database window.

3   Double-Click *Create form by using wizard*.

The first dialog of the Form Wizard opens.

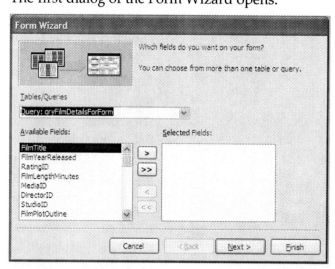

4   Choose qryFilmDetailsForForm as the data source for the form and select the following fields in the following order:

FilmTitle
FilmYearReleased
RatingID
FilmLengthMinutes
MediaID
DirectorID
StudioID
FilmPlotOutline
FilmReview
FilmFrontCover

Session1f

5   Click the Next button, accept the columnar form layout and click the Next button once more.

6   Accept the Standard style and click the Next button.

7   Rename the form frmFilm and click the Finish button.

The Wizard created form is displayed.

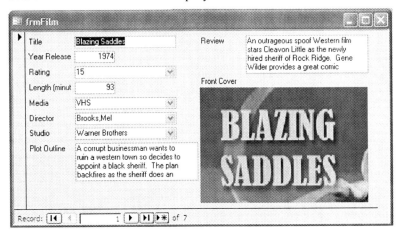

The form isn't great but it isn't bad either. The only obvious major error is the Front Cover graphic that is only partially displayed.

note

The Frame object's *Size Mode* property defaults to Clip. This means that the image will be shown at full resolution but only a partial image will display if space does not permit.

By changing the property to Zoom it will automatically scale to fill the space allocated for it on the form.

8   Change the Front Cover graphic so that it scales.

Switch to Design View and then Right-click in the part of the form where you saw the graphic displayed (it is invisible until you right-click it). Choose Options from the shortcut menu and change the Bound Object Frame's *Size Mode* property: to Zoom.

9   Switch to Form View and try out your new form.

It is actually quite impressive already and we haven't done any work at all yet!

Lesson 1-9: Improve the prototype form for keyboard input

The Wizard had done a fair job but we need to refine its work a little in order to move towards a professional form.

1   Add a hot key to the Title label.

Hot keys are keyboard shortcuts so that a user can quickly navigate to any field without using a mouse.

Right click on the form's Title label control, choose Properties from the short cut menu, and re-name the caption property from Title to &Title. Change to Form View and note the underline underneath the T of Title.

Click into a different field and then press <Alt>+<T> on your keyboard. Note how the focus immediately changes to the Title field.

2   Add hot keys to all of the other label controls.

Note that for the Review label there is a problem as the letter R has already been used as a hotkey in the Rating field. The solution is to change the caption to Re&view in order to make the v key the hotkey for this label.

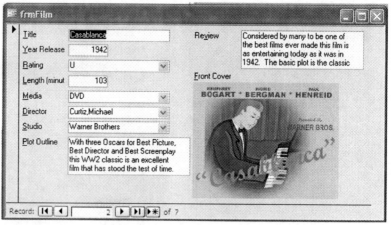

3   Change the label Length (minutes) to Length (mins).

Change the caption property of the label control to Length (mins).

Even though this does, strictly speaking, break our Cradle to the Grave naming convention it can be excused as it saves a lot of time in moving all of the controls and remains unambiguous.

Length (mins)   103

4   Test the form's tab order.

Try tabbing through the fields on the form. For this form the tab order is probably already perfect but if it needs changing this can

Session1g

be done by changing to Design View and selecting View→Tab Order from the main menu.

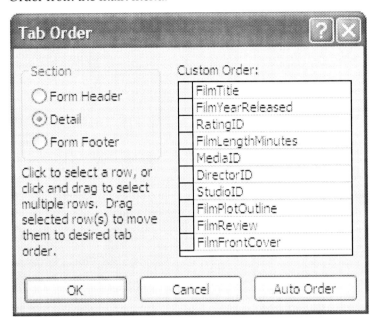

We now have a reasonably professional-looking form

Lesson 1-10: Create a simple report using a wizard

As with forms, it is always a great idea to begin a report by using the wizard and then to further refine the report using more advanced techniques.

1   Make a copy of the qryFilmDetails query called qryFilmDetailsForFilmListReport.

Right-click the qryFilmDetails query in the query window and choose Copy. Right-click again and choose Paste to copy the query. Right-click the copied query and choose Rename to rename the query.

2   Click the Reports object in the Database window.

3   Double-Click Create report by using wizard.

The first dialog of the Report Wizard opens.

4   Use qryFilmDetailsForFilmListReport as the query that will underpin the report.

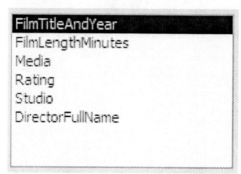

5   Select the following fields (in the order shown) for the new report:

> FilmTitleAndYear
> FilmLengthMinutes
> Media
> Rating
> Studio
> DirectorFullName

6   Click the Next button and stay with the default choice *By Film.*

Session1h

7   Click the Next button but do not add any grouping levels.

8   Click the Next button. There's no need to set a sort order as that has already been done within the query.

9   Click the Next button. Stay with a tabular layout but change the orientation to Landscape.

10   Click the Next button and stay with the default Corporate style.

11   Click the Next button and re-name the report to rptFilmList.

12   Click the Finish button and view the finished report.

rptFilmList

FilmTitleAndYear	Length (minutes)	Media	Rating	Studio	DirectorFullName
Blazing Saddles(1974)	93	VHS	15	Warner Brothers	Brooks,Mel
Casablanca(1942)	103	DVD	U	Warner Brothers	Curtiz,Michael
Get Carter(1971)	111	DVD	18	Metro-Glodwin-Mayer (MGM)	Hodges,Mike
Get Carter(2000)	102	DVD	15	Warner Brothers	Kay,Stephen T.
Gone With The Wind(1939)	233	DVD	PG	Metro-Glodwin-Mayer (MGM)	Fleming,Victor
Interview With The Vampire(19	122	VHS	18	Warner Brothers	Jordan,Neil
It's A Wonderful Life(1947)	132	VHS	U	Republic Pictures	Capra,Frank

13   Change to Design View and fix up the title and labels so that your report displays as follows:

Film List

Title And Year	Length (minutes)	Media	Rating	Studio	Director
Blazing Saddles(1974)	93	VHS	15	Warner Brothers	Brooks,Mel
Casablanca(1942)	103	DVD	U	Warner Brothers	Curtiz,Michael
Get Carter(1971)	111	DVD	18	Metro-Glodwin-Mayer (MGM)	Hodges,Mike
Get Carter(2000)	102	DVD	15	Warner Brothers	Kay,Stephen T.
Gone With The Wind(1939)	233	DVD	PG	Metro-Glodwin-Mayer (MGM)	Fleming,Victor
Interview With The Vampire(19	122	VHS	18	Warner Brothers	Jordan,Neil
It's A Wonderful Life(1947)	132	VHS	U	Republic Pictures	Capra,Frank

It would be possible to tidy the report up a little more but we do have a credible and useful report so we'll leave it there and declare the report complete.

Session 1: Exercise

In this exercise you'll quickly create an application for managing a telephone contact log. The application will honour all of the rules learned during this session and also restated in *Appendix A-The Rules.*

1   Create a new blank database named *Exercise1.*

2   Create the Contact table.

Create and name your table (don't worry about the field names yet… that's coming in Q3) and then check the answer to confirm that your table is correctly named (slide the page slightly to the left to view the Q2 answer).

3   Add fields to your new table to store a primary key along with the following information:

First Name, Last Name, Telephone Number.

Set the *Caption* property for each field to the correct value and set an appropriate data type.

Check that your fields were correctly named, captioned and typed (slide the page a little more to the left to view the Q3 answer).

4   You want to record all telephone calls made to each contact. Create a new table to store telephone calls and give it an appropriate name.

Add a primary key, a foreign key to reference the Contact table and a memo field to store details of all calls made to each client. Name each field and its caption property appropriately.

Check your work agrees with the Q4 answer.

5   Set the foreign key (the reference to the Contact primary key in the Call table) to be a lookup field.

6   Use the wizard to generate a form from each table. Name the forms correctly.

Check that your form names agree with the Q6 answer.

7   Set hot keys for each label control on each form.

8   Test your application.

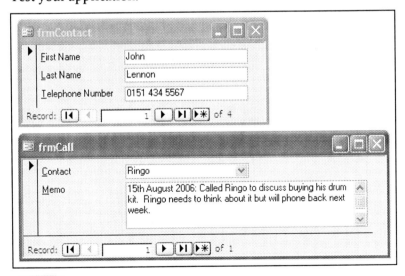

Exercise1End

Session 1: Exercise answers

Q 6	Q 4	Q 3	Q 2
Form name should be the same as the table name but with a prefix of frm. Form names should thus be frmContact and frmCall.	A good name for the table would be Call as TelephoneCall is a little wordy (though still correct). The primary key can then only be called CallId with a data type of AutoNumber. The last field should be called CallMemo (or similar) with a caption of Memo. The Foreign Key should have exactly the same name as the primary key in the Contact table—ContactId. It should have the data type of Number and a caption of Contact.	The primary key should have been named: ContactID (the table name post fixed with ID for the primary key) with data type of AutoNumber The three data fields should have been named: ContactFirstName, ContactLastName and ContactTelephoneNumer as field names should be prefixed by the table name and should never be abbreviated. The captions should have been identical to the field names but without the table prefix and with a space between each word: First Name, Last Name, and Telephone Number. The data type of the ContactFirstName, ContactLastName and ContactTelephoneNumber fields should be text. You may be forgiven for thinking that *Number* would be an appropriate data type for the *ContactTelephoneNumber* field but this would cause problems with telephone numbers beginning with a zero as leading zeros would not be stored or displayed on the form.	You should have named your table Contact and not Contacts as table names should always be in the singular and not be prefixed.

Session Two: Adding Advanced Features Using Wizards

> You have to crawl before you can walk,
> You have to learn to walk before you can run.
>
> *Proverbs, unknown authors*

When I was at school everybody wanted to be a rock musician. Unfortunately few wanted to learn to play a guitar or keyboards. Learning any new subject is a little like this. We want it all and we want it now.

In this chapter we're going to have a taste of being an instant rock star by creating some VBA code using the switchboard, command button and combo box wizards. Quite how the wizard is creating the code, and what the code means, will still remain a mystery but being able to do something useful with VBA at once might be more fun than going straight into programming theory.

In later sessions, after you have learned the VBA programming language, we'll re-visit the features added in this session and examine the VBA code written by the wizards in minute detail. We'll even find ways of improving the wizard's work!

Session Objectives

By the end of this session you will be able to:

- ▓ Add a switchboard form using a Wizard
- ▓ Add a command button using a Wizard
- ▓ Add a combo box lookup feature using a Wizard

Session2

Lesson 2-1: Add a switchboard to the application using the Switchboard Wizard

Microsoft has given the name *Switchboard* to a special form that can be used to provide a simple user interface for Access applications.

When you've completed this course you'll probably want to break free of the Switchboard Wizard as it is very simple to create a better switchboard from scratch once you understand a little more about Access VBA. For now we'll use the Wizard to quickly and automatically generate the code needed for the Switchboard.

note

Until the early 90's the switchboard type of user interface was the norm for older "green screen" type DOS applications.

With the wide acceptance of Windows 3.0 users became more used to the drop-down menu/toolbar type of user interface. This type of user interface is used by all Microsoft Office applications.

Switchboards are easy to program and convenient but not often seen in contemporary applications.

In a later session we will convert the application to a modern drop-down menu/toolbar interface.

1   Create a new switchboard.

Select Tools→Database Utilities→Switchboard Manager from the main menu. When you are asked whether you want to create a Switchboard click the Yes button.

The Switchboard Manager dialog is displayed.

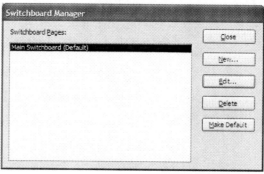

2   Add buttons to the switchboard to enable users to access your form and report.

Click the Switchboard Manager's Edit… button. The *Edit Switchboard Page* dialog is displayed.

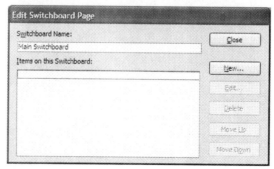

3   Click the New… button to add a button that will display the Film List report.

Session2

Enter *Preview the Film List report* for the Text, *Open Report* for the Command and *rptFilmList* for the Report to open.

4   Click the OK button and then the New... button once more to add a button to enable the user to add new films.

Enter *Add a new film* for the Text, *Open Form in Add Mode* for the Command and *frmFilm* for the Form to open.

5   Click the OK button and then the New... button once more to add a button to enable the user to edit existing films.

Enter *Edit an existing film* for the Text, *Open Form in Edit Mode* for the Command and *frmFilm* for the Form to Edit

6   Click the *OK* button and then the *Close* button twice to generate the switchboard form.

7   Test your new switchboard form.

A new form has been generated called *Switchboard*. Open the form and try out the switchboard.

Lesson 2-2: Add a command button to a form using a wizard

The buttons on the switchboard form are objects called *Command Buttons*. We're going to add a command button to our frmFilm form that will add functionality normally only available to VBA programmers.

1 Open the frmFilm form in Design View.

2 Make a little space in the Form Footer area for the command button.

Position the mouse over the bottom of the Form Footer bar and drag slightly downwards.

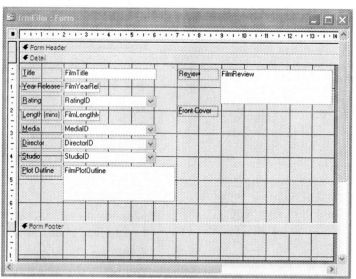

3 If the Toolbox isn't displayed click the Toolbox button on the Form Design Toolbar to display it.

4 Make sure that the Control Wizard is enabled.

Note that there is a button called the *Control Wizards Button* at the top of the Toolbox. Make sure that this button is pressed in. There is no good reason to ever disable the Control Wizards by not keeping this button depressed.

5 Add a Command Button to the Form Footer area.

Click once on the Command Button icon in the Toolbox and then click and drag to draw a Command Button in the Form Footer area of your form. The Command Button Wizard appears.

6 Give the button the ability to delete records.

Select the *Record Operations* category and the *Delete Record* action. This will give the button the ability to delete the current record.

Session2a

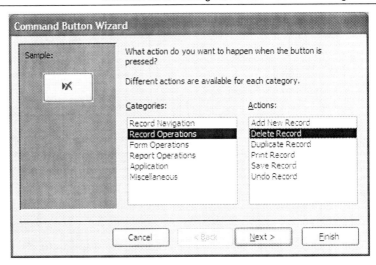

7   Click the Next button and select the Text option button. Change the text to De&lete as the D hotkey would clash with the Director hotkey.

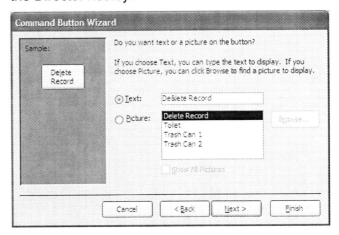

8   Click the Next button and correctly name your new control cmdDelete.

9   Test your new command button without deleting any records.

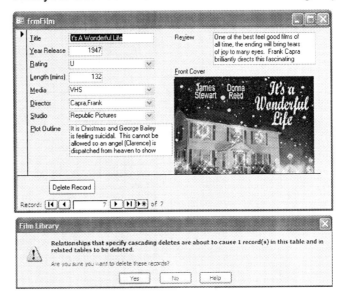

Lesson 2-3: Add a combo box lookup feature to a form using a wizard

A form needs to be able to locate a specific record quickly. We're ultimately going to produce an application that can be intuitively used without any Access skills so a simple method to find records is required. Fortunately there's a very easy way to do this without having to write any VBA code by using yet another Wizard.

1   Open the frmFilm form in Design View and open up a little space in the Form Header area.

   Position the mouse at the top of the Detail bar and drag downwards to create some space.

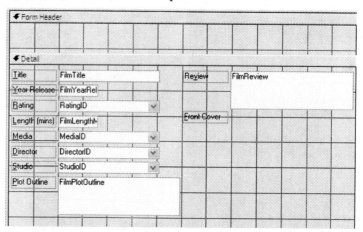

2   Add a Combo Box control to the Form Header area.

   The Combo Box Wizard appears.

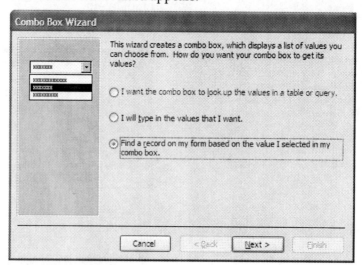

3   Choose the *Find a record on my form based on the value I selected in my combo box* option button and click the Next button.

   The field selection dialog appears.

Session2b

Important

If you didn't select the primary key (FilmID) as the first field for the Combo Box Wizard – and then hide it later – things would still work fine.

So why did we bother?

We bothered because the combo box will work faster and more efficiently as a result.

With your current understanding of Access it is not possible to explain why this is the case but later, when you've mastered VBA, we'll analyse the wizard-generated code and all will become clear.

important

A generally accepted (and extremely important) database design rule is that primary keys should always be meaningless (ie automatically set to an arbitrary value with the AutoNumber data type).

Because the primary key is meaningless it always makes sense to hide it from the user.

This rule (and others) is listed in Appendix A: The Rules.

4   Select the FilmId and FilmTitleAndYear fields and then click the Next button.

The style dialog appears.

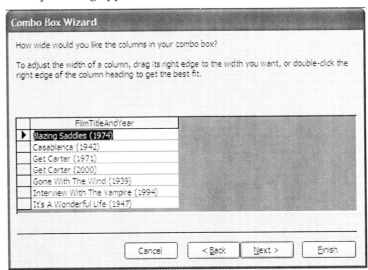

5   Select an appropriate width for the combo box and make sure that the primary key is hidden.

Position the mouse cursor over the right hand side of the *FilmTitleAndYear* gray bar and then click and drag right or left to re-size. Hide the primary key by dragging the intersection of FilmId and FilmTitleAndYear completely to the left and then click the Next button.

The label text dialog appears.

6   Give the combo box a label of: *Find Film:* and then click the Finish button.

7   Test the new control.

Return to Form View and select a film from the combo box's drop down list. The relevant film details are displayed in the form.

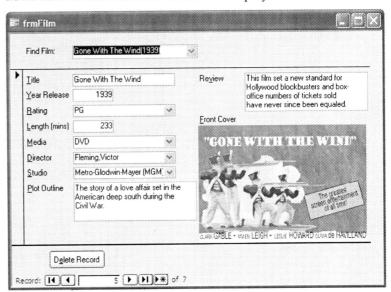

Session 2: Exercise

In this exercise you'll use the command button Wizard to provide an alternative set of navigation buttons for a copy of the application you have built to date.

1   Make a copy of your *FilmLibrary.mdb* file and re-name it *Exercise2.mdb* (there is also an *Exercise2Start.mdb* file available for download from our web site).

2   Open Exercise2.mdb.

3   Open frmFilm in Design View and add a command button to the form.

4   When the wizard dialog appears see if you can work out which *Category* and *Action* is needed to make the button navigate to the first record.

        Only if you are unable to work out the right *Category* and *Action* slide the page slightly to the left to view the Q3 answer.

5   Click the Next button, give your new button the *GoTo First 2* picture and click the Next button.

6   Name the button cmdGoToFirst and click the Finish button.

7   Now follow on with another four buttons so that you have replaced the functionality of the standard record navigation bar.

        Only if you cannot work out the correct Category and Action for any of the buttons slide the page slightly to the left to view the Q6 answer.

        Your completed navigation bar should now look like this:

8   Change the form property: *Record Selectors* to No.

        Only if you can not work out how to do this slide the page slightly to the left to view the Q7 answer.

        Your form should now look something like this:

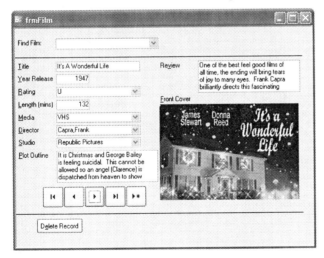

Exercise2Start   Exercise2End

Session 2: Exercise answers

Q 8	Q 7	Q 4
Right-click the square ■ at the top left corner of the form and select Properties from the short-cut menu. Change the property *Navigation Buttons* from Yes to No. This will make the standard navigation buttons disappear.	For Navigation buttons use **Category**: Navigation and **Actions:** Go To First Record ⏮, Go To Previous Record ◀, Go To Next Record ▶, and Go To Last Record ⏭. For the *Add New* button ▶* use **Category:** Record Operations and **Action:** Add New Record.	**Category:** Record Navigation **Action:** Go To First Record

Session Three: The Object-Orientated Paradigm

> When I ask you for one virtue, you present me with a swarm of them, which are in your keeping. Suppose that I carry on the figure of the swarm, and ask of you, what is the nature of the bee? And you answer that there are many kinds of bees. And I reply: But do bees differ as bees, because there are many and different kinds of them; or are they not rather to be distinguished by some other quality, as for example beauty, size, or shape? How would you answer me?
>
> *Socrates as transcribed by Plato (Meno) 399 BC*

When Socrates proclaimed that all bees are "just the same but different" perhaps he was talking about objects but was just a little ahead of his time.

While a (now obscure) language called Simula established most of the key concepts of Object Orientated programming in 1967, object orientated programming only became mainstream with Bjarne Stroustroup's definition of the C++ programming language in 1985. Had computers been around in Socrates' time we might have been using these techniques about 2,400 years earlier!

In the last session we had a taste of running before we could crawl. In the next two sessions we'll learn enough about the Access Object model and the VBA Programming language to be able to crawl, or perhaps even walk in a slightly wobbly way.

This chapter begins by teaching you the extremely simple concepts behind objects and their three ways of interfacing with the outside world: properties, methods and events. We'll even attach a little VBA code to an event.

You will end this session with a full appreciation of what objects are, what they can do, and what an object model is.

Session Objectives

By the end of this session you will be able to:

- Understand object properties
- Understand object methods
- Understand object events
- Understand some of the objects in the Access object model

Session3

Lesson 3-1: Understand properties

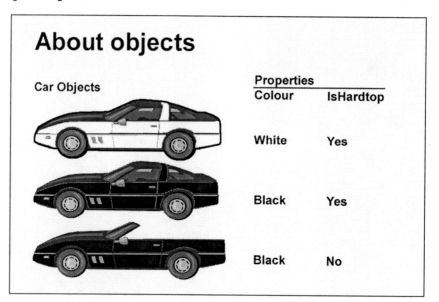

About objects

What are properties?

The slide above shows three cars. We can recognise them all as cars but there are some things that are different about them.

In object-speak we would say that the cars have different properties.

We can think of each as being a car object. If I were to telephone you and say "I bought a new car" you wouldn't know what color it was or whether it was a hard top—but you would still have an abstract idea of what was sitting in my driveway.

To better visualise the car you would have to ask a few questions like:

- Is it a convertible?

- What color is it?

To relate this to Access consider a Form object. Form objects have a *Caption* property that puts the name of the form into the top blue bar.

If you added enough properties to the *Car* object you would eventually be able to precisely describe every car on the planet.

This would solve Socrates' bee problem too!

Session3

Objects contain objects

The car object contains a windscreen object. It also has four wheel objects that are identical (or at least very similar). In object-speak we would say that the car object contains a windscreen object and a collection of wheel objects.

The Access *Form* object contains a collection of control objects (such as command buttons and text boxes).

How properties are set for controls

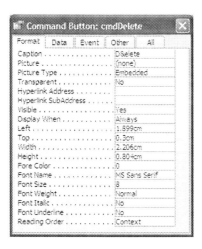

1   Examine the properties of the cmdDelete command button on the frmFilm form.

Open the form in Design View, right-click the cmdDelete button and choose Properties from the shortcut menu.

You can probably figure out what most of the properties mean.

note

Properties can be set both using the properties dialog and via VBA code.

For the moment we'll only use the properties dialog method but when we know a little more about the VBA programming language we'll be setting some properties using VBA code.

Lesson 3-2: Understand methods

What are methods?

As well as having properties to describe an object some objects have certain functionality too. Let's consider a Car object. We may have precisely described it by setting properties such as Color, NumberOfSeats and FuelType but what is the car for? Is it a film prop, a paperweight, or does it actually do something?

The things objects can do are called methods.

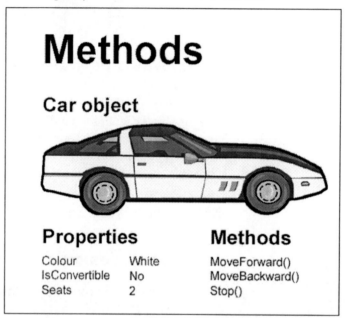

All cars have several methods such as StartEngine, MoveForward, Stop, SteerLeft and SteerRight. Some cars have methods that are not common to all cars such as StartAirConditioner or EnableCruiseControl.

note

Some programmers prefer the term *Parameter* instead of *Argument*. Both are correct.

Methods may be modified by arguments

Access objects have methods too. For example a Combo Box object has an AddItem method.

Simply invoking the MoveForward method of the Car object wouldn't really be enough. To more precisely tell the car what to do we might want to say:

Move forward three metres.

In order to do this we'd need to invoke the MoveForward method along with some instructions telling the car how to move forwards. These instructions are called parameters or arguments. The actual MoveForward() method call would more likely be something like this:

MoveForward(3)

Session3

Where the argument 3 represents the distance to move forwards in metres.

Examples of methods available in Access objects

A method with no parameters

Methods do not have to have parameters. A good example of a very useful method is the Form object's Requery method. Invoking the Requery method will execute the SQL query that underpins the form and will then update all of the controls on the form to reflect the current state of the data.

This could be very useful in a multi-user environment when the user wanted to be sure that the data displayed on the screen was completely up to date.

A method with parameters

The Combo Box object has a method that allows items to be added to it. This is intuitively named the *AddItem* method.

Clearly the *AddItem* method must have some parameters in order to tell the Combo Box object something about the item to be added.

The method actually has two parameters. The first is the text that will be displayed in the combo box and the second is an optional parameter to indicate the position in the list.

For Example:

```
AddItem( "London")
AddItem( "Glasgow")
```

Would result in a combo box with two entries, the first would be London and the second Glasgow.

```
AddItem( "London", 1 )
AddItem( "Glasgow", 0)
```

Would result in a combo box with two entries, the first would be Glasgow and the second London.

Lesson 3-3: Understand events

What are events?

Consider a telephone. Somebody could call the telephone at any time. The telephone doesn't know when it is going to happen, or even whether it will ever happen at all.

Suppose somebody does call, the telephone might respond by ringing its bell.

In object-speak we'd say that the telephone object had responded to its SomebodyCalling event by invoking its RingBell method.

1   Open a new blank database and save it as VBACode.mdb.

2   Create a new form in Design View and save it as frmTest.

3   Add a command button to your new form dismissing the Command Button Wizard by clicking its Cancel button.

4   Set some of the Command Button's properties.

A Command Button (and every other control) is an object and will have its own set of properties, methods and events. It's important that you get into this mindset in order to understand how VBA and Access interact.

To view the Command Button's property sheet right-click it and select Properties from the shortcut menu.

Set the Command Button's Name property to *cmdPressMe* and the Caption property to *&Press Me*.

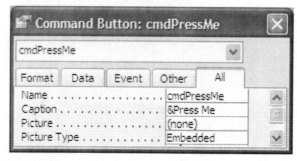

Let's now consider an event that might happen in the life of a command button.

The most important thing that can happen to the command button is that somebody might click it. This is referred to in object terminology as the command button's *Click* event.

5   Right-click the command button and choose Code Builder from the shortcut menu.

The Choose Builder dialog appears.

Session3

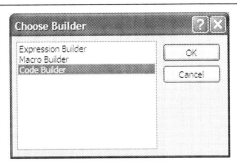

6   Choose Code Builder from the dialog.

The VBA editor appears with code for the Command Button's Click event handler displayed.

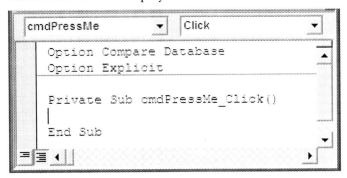

The command button does have other events but the Click event is shown by default as it is the most important event for this control.

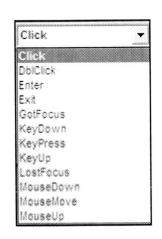

7   Browse the Command Button's other events.

There's plenty of other less obvious things that can happen to a command button. In all there are twelve events.

Open the VBA editor and select the pulldown list arrow at the top right of the code window. Browse the possible events for a Command Button. You should be able to guess what most of them mean.

8   Add the following code to the Command Button's Click event:

```
Private Sub cmdPressMe_Click()

Beep

End Sub
```

9   Test the Command Button's event handler.

Close the Visual Basic editor and display the form in Form View.

Click the button (make sure that your computer's sound is switched on). When you click the button the Click event is triggered. The code you added causes the computer to beep.

Lesson 3-4: Understand the Access object model

> Greater bugs have little bugs
> Upon their backs to bite 'em
>
> Little bugs have lesser bugs
> And so on ad infinitum
>
> *May Louise Cooper, "Friendly Beetles", (1916)*

About object hierarchies

We have already seen how a Car object can contain other objects (such as a windscreen object).

Objects can also contain object collections of similar objects. In the earlier example the Car object had a collection of Wheel objects. The wheel objects did not necessarily have the same properties—for example there may have been wider tyres fitted on the rear wheels.

Object models express the concept of a hierarchy evident in May Louise Cooper's observation above. Each of her bugs is connected to another bug higher up in the hierarchy.

The Car object model

Before considering the Access object model let's consider the Car object model that we've been discussing. Here it is:

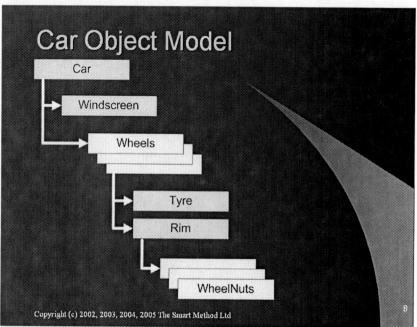

- A Car object contains a Windscreen object and a collection of Wheel objects.

Session3

- Each wheel object contains a Rim object, and a Tyre object.

- Each Rim object contains a collection of WheelNut objects.

The Access object model

The Access object model contains a little over fifty objects. We're going to ease you gently into the model by introducing new objects as we use them during this course. We've already identified three of the most important objects.

Here's the object model as we know it so far :

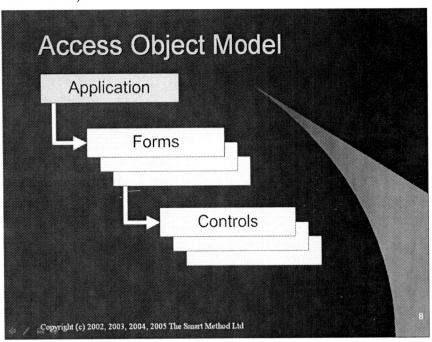

Microsoft always name collections in the plural and single objects in the singular. It is thus obvious that the Forms item in the above diagram is actually a collection of Form objects.

From the object model above it is clear that :

- One Application object may contain zero, one or more Form objects.

- Each Form object may contain zero, one or more Control objects.

Microsoft's object model diagram

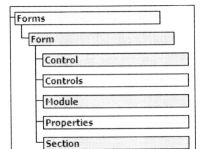

If you type *Access Object Model* into the help dialog you'll be able to view the entire Access object model.

Microsoft use color coding to indicate collections of objects, and there's a few objects that you might not recognize, but from what you have learned in this section, and your existing Access skills, you will be able to understand the purpose of many of the objects.

Session 3: Exercise

1   Consider a Head object. The Head object contains several single objects and several object Collections. Which of the following are single Objects and which are part of an Object Collection?

Eye   □ Single Object   □ Collection

Nose   □ Single Object   □ Collection

Hair   □ Single Object   □ Collection

Ear   □ Single Object   □ Collection

Mouth   □ Single Object   □ Collection

Tongue   □ Single Object   □ Collection

Tooth   □ Single Object   □ Collection

If you are having difficulty with the concept of single objects and object collections slide the page slightly to the left for some help.

2   Consider a Car object. Which of the following are Properties, which are Methods and which are Events?

Color   □ Property   □ Method   □ Event

MoveForward   □ Property   □ Method   □ Event

Start   □ Property   □ Method   □ Event

HitByStone   □ Property   □ Method   □ Event

BreakDown   □ Property   □ Method   □ Event

Make   □ Property   □ Method   □ Event

Model   □ Property   □ Method   □ Event

Stop   □ Property   □ Method   □ Event

If you are having difficulty with the concept of properties, methods and events slide the page slightly to the left for some help.

3   Name two properties, methods and events that a person object might have.

Slide the page to the left if you need to view some sample answers or to confirm that yours are reasonable.

Session 3: Exercise answers

Q 3	Q 2	Q 1
Some examples: **Properties:** Height, Weight, Age, Nationality, BirthPlace, HairColor. **Methods:** Walk, Run, Swim, TurnLeft, TurnRight, Whistle, Shout, Talk, Sleep. **Events:** Hungry, Tired, Thirsty, Hot, Cold, Sick.	A Property often describes an object's physical appearance. For example a *Car* object has a *Color* property. A *Method* is something an object can do. For example a *Car* object has a *Stop* method. An *Event* is something that may happen unexpectedly in the life of an object. For example a *Car* object may encounter a *HitByStone* event.	An example of a single object is a *Nose* object because a *Head* can only have one *Nose*. When there are two or more very similar (though not necessarily identical) objects they are bundled into an object collection. For example: a Head object contains a collection of *Tooth* objects.

Session Four: An Introduction To VBA

> When I was a kid in school, I learned to read and write
> And every morning in the hall, we sang with all our might
>
> School days are happy days but then you have to go
> And it only takes two hours to put down all you need to know.
>
> *Children's Song by Neil Innes*

Visual Basic is the most widely used language in the world for building business applications.

Neil Innes assertion works fine with Visual Basic. It really does only take two hours to learn all you need to know to write solid, professional code.

We used to teach the entire VBA language in one session but after years of running our VBA courses in both Excel and Access flavours, decided that this was too ambitious.

This session will get you started in VBA. The code you'll write won't be professional grade yet but you'll be well versed in the basics and be able to write some elementary code. We'll also introduce the debug tools in this session. It may seem odd to learn debug tools before you've even understood the language but you'll find them very useful as you learn more advanced language elements.

The session that follows this one ("Professional Grade VBA") will build upon the basic skills learned in this session and add some vital techniques to make your code professional and robust. This will allow you to begin to do some really useful things with VBA.

Session Objectives

By the end of this session you will be able to:

- Understand subs
- Step through code
- Understand stepover, step into and step out
- Understand variables
- Use the immediate window to view and change variable contents
- Use the locals window to view and change variable contents

Session4

Lesson 4-1: Understand subs

note

Sometimes you'll hear the term Sub Routine used instead of Sub Procedure. You'll also hear some people refer to Sub Procedures as simply Procedures.

None of this terminology is incorrect; we just have many different words that refer to exactly the same thing.

We will simply use the word *Sub* in this book.

Most real-world tasks can be broken down into smaller tasks. In programming we call tasks *procedures*. Procedures can be split into Sub procedures. Consider the procedure of opening your front door. It can be broken down into several sub-procedures:

■   Insert key

■   Turn key anti-clockwise

■   Push door inwards

■   Remove key

■   Close door

Defining procedures in VBA code

In VBA we cannot leave spaces in procedure names so we would name the above sub-procedures:

InsertKey, TurnKeyAntiClockwise, PushDoorInwards, RemoveKey and CloseDoor.

In VBA code we use the keywords *Sub* and *End Sub* to de-lineate procedures and sub-procedures. There's no distinct difference between a Sub-procedure and a Procedure as they are all de-lineated by the Sub... End Sub statements.

Most VBA programmers refer to sub-procedures simply as *Subs*. The InsertKey sub would thus be typed into the editor as follows:

```
Sub InsertKey()

' InsertKey VBA code will go here

End Sub
```

Note two more things about the above code. We have added parenthesis after the Sub Procedure's name and also a single quotation mark in front of the comment *InsertKey VBA code will go here*. Comments in code are ignored by VBA and can be used to add comments to describe what your code does and how it works.

tip

Always use the Upper/Lower Case naming convention for Sub names (as used in TurnKeyAntiClockwise)

Never use underscores in your own sub names and then it will always be clear which subs are event handlers.

Never, ever, abbreviate words, for example do not use sub names such as TrnKeyAntiClkwse.

These rules (and the reasons for them) are listed in *Appendix A: The Rules*.

Calling procedures in VBA code

To execute all of the sub procedures we have discussed and open the door we would call the subs in sequence like this:

```
Sub OpenDoor()

Call InsertKey
Call TurnKeyAntiClockwise
Call PushDoorInwards
Call RemoveKey
Call CloseDoor

End Sub
```

Session4

1   Open the VBACode.mdb database created in the last chapter (if not already open).

2   Open the frmTest form's event handler for the cmdPressMe button's Click event.

Open frmTest in Design View. Right click on the Command Button and select Build Event from the shortcut menu. The code for the Command Button's Click event is displayed in the code editor.

note

The MsgBox() call is actually to a special type of sub called a function.

Functions can be regarded as being the same as a sub except that they are able to return a value. The MsgBox sometimes returns a value to indicate which message box button was pressed (some MsgBox's have a Yes and No button).

We'll learn all about functions in a later lesson.

3   Add a new Sub procedure called ThankYouMessage.

Do this by adding the following code:

```
Sub ThankYouMessage()
End Sub
```

4   Remove the Beep statement from the cmdPressMe_Click Sub procedure and add the following code to the ThankYouMessage() Sub procedure:

```
Sub ThankYouMessage()
Beep
Call MsgBox("Thank you for pressing me")
End Sub
```

In its present form the code will not do a thing when the command button is pressed. We need to call the ThankYouMessage sub procedure from the cmdPressMe_Click() event handler.

tip

You do not have to use the Call keyword when calling a sub or function but most professional programmers would always use this coding style as it makes code far more readable by allowing arguments (if any) to be contained by parenthesis.

For example:-

Call MsgBox("Hello")

Instead of:-

MsgBox "Hello"

If you are programming in a team environment it is useful to agree common coding standards such as this so that each member of the team is able to immediately understand other team member's code.

This rule (and others) is listed in *Appendix A: The Rules*.

5   Add a call to the ThankYouMessage sub procedure to the cmdPressMe_Click event handler.

```
Private Sub cmdPressMe_Click()
Call ThankYouMessage
End Sub
```

6   Test the command button.

Display the form in Form View. When you click the command button you should now hear a beep and see the message.

Full code listing

```
Private Sub cmdPressMe_Click()
Call ThankYouMessage
End Sub

Sub ThankYouMessage()
Beep
Call MsgBox("Thank you for pressing me")
End Sub
```

Lesson 4-2: Step through code

Whenever we write code we're likely to make mistakes. Programmers call mistakes *bugs* for interesting historical reasons (see sidebar).

Now is a great time to introduce one of the VBA Debug tools. The debug tools help you to track down the source of any problems that are encountered when you test your code.

There are many debug tools and we'll be learning about all of them in future lessons. This lesson introduces one of the most useful tools: the ability to step through code.

1   Open the VBACode.mdb database created in the last chapter (if not already open).

2   Open the event handler for the cmdPressMe button's Click event.

The Code Editor window is displayed.

3   Enable the Debug toolbar if it is not already displayed.

You can do this by selecting View→Toolbars→Debug from the main menu.

4   Add a breakpoint on the line *Call ThankYouMessage*.

Click anywhere in the text *Call ThankYouMessage* and then click the Toggle Breakpoint button 🤚 on the Debug toolbar to insert a breakpoint. The selected text is highlighted.

Try clicking the Toggle Breakpoint button 🤚 twice more to remove and add the breakpoint.

Try clicking in the margin (where you see the brown circle) and note that this method can also be used to toggle breakpoints.

5   Return to Access by clicking the View Access button 🖉 on the Code Editor's standard toolbar and then change frmTest from *Design View* to *Form View*.

6   Click the cmdPressMe command button.

You are transferred to the code editor with code execution halted at the breakpoint.

Session4a

7 Click the Step Into button ⬛ on the Debug Toolbar twice.

The code steps into the ThankYouMessage sub procedure header and then to the line saying Beep.

```
Private Sub ThankYouMessage()
    Beep
    Call MsgBox("Thank you for pressing me")
End Sub
```

8 Click the Step Into button ⬛ on the Debug Toolbar once more

An audible Beep is heard as the code executes and the code steps to the next line *Call MsgBox…*

```
Private Sub ThankYouMessage()
    Beep
    Call MsgBox("Thank you for pressing me")
End Sub
```

9 Click the Step Into button ⬛ on the Debug Toolbar once more

The message box is displayed. Clicking the OK button on the message box steps the code to the next line *End Sub.*

```
Private Sub ThankYouMessage()
    Beep
    Call MsgBox("Thank you for pressing me")
End Sub
```

10 Click the Step Into button ⬛ on the Debug Toolbar once more

The code moves to the *End Sub* statement from the calling function cmdPressMe_Click.

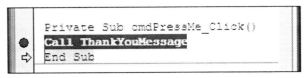

11 Click the Step Into button ⬛ on the Debug Toolbar once more

Nothing happens as all code has executed.

12 Remove the breakpoint.

Lesson 4-3: Understand step over and step out

1   Begin in exactly the same way as the previous lesson by setting a breakpoint at the line *Call ThankYouMessage*.

2   Return to the form and Click the cmdPressMe command button.

You are transferred to the code editor with code execution halted at the breakpoint.

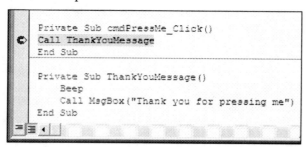

3   Click the Step Over button 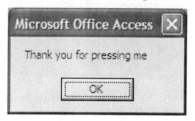 on the debug toolbar.

An audible Beep is heard as the code in ThankYouMessage executes and the Message Box is immediately displayed.

Microsoft Office Access ✕

Thank you for pressing me

OK

This happened because the code in the ThankYouMessage sub will execute as normal and will not be stepped through as we requested that VBA *stepped over* the subroutine.

Click the OK button and execution halts at *End Sub* in the cmdPressMe_Click event handler.

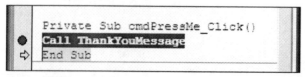

This is very useful when you want to examine the way code is executed in a single sub but have no interest in the code within any other subs that it may call.

Session4a

4   Click the Step Over button 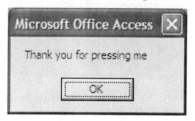 (or Step Into button) on the Debug Toolbar.

Nothing happens as all code has executed. In this case *Step Into* and *Step Over* will result in exactly the same action.

5 Click the cmdPressMe command button.

You are transferred to the code editor with code execution halted at the breakpoint.

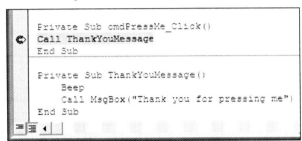

6 Click the Step Into button  on the Debug Toolbar twice.

The code steps into the ThankYouMessage sub procedure header and then to the line saying Beep.

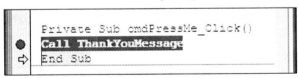

7 Click the Step Out button ⮤ on the Debug Toolbar once more.

An audible Beep is heard as the code executes and the message box is immediately displayed.

Microsoft Office Access [X]

Thank you for pressing me

OK

8 Click the OK button on the displayed message box.

Code execution is now halted at the next line of code in the cmdPressMe_Click event handler. The Step Out button has executed all remaining code in the ThankYouMessage sub procedure without stopping and then paused on the next executable line of the calling sub procedure—cmdPressMe_Click.

```
Private Sub cmdPressMe_Click()
Call ThankYouMessage
End Sub
```

Step Out is very useful when you are no longer interested in the remaining code within the current sub but want to examine how the remainder of the code in the calling sub will execute.

Lesson 4-4: Understand variables

note

Why the strange variable name?

You may have thought that we would call a variable that will store a First Name simply *FirstName* rather than *strFirstName*.

While VBA wouldn't complain about a variable named *FirstName* we use the prefix *str* in order to show that the variable contains string (text) information rather than, for example, a date or a number.

You'll learn more about the reason why this is a good idea when we cover data types more thoroughly in a later lesson.

Variable naming conventions are all documented in *Appendix A: The Rules*.

What are variables?

A variable is a container that is able to store data of any type in memory.

Every *variable* has a *data type*. For example a variable may be a number, text or a date.

Suppose we have two variables called *strFirstName* and *strLastName*.

Look at the following VBA code:

```
strFirstName = "Freddie"
strLastName = "Mercury"
strFullName = strFirstName & " " & strLastName
```

The strFullName variable now contains the text *Freddie Mercury*. Note the concatenation operator (&) used to append a space (" ") onto the text *Freddie* and the text *Mercury* after the space.

1   If it is not already open, open the VBACode.mdb database.

2   Open the frmTest form in Design View.

3   Open the VBA Editor.

When the form is in Design View you will notice a Code Button on the top toolbar. Clicking this button will take you straight to the Code Editor and is quicker than right-clicking the command button and selecting Build Event from the shortcut menu.

4   Add the following code to the ThankYouMessage sub procedure:

```
strMessage = "Thank you for pressing me."
```

5   Replace the message text in the MsgBox function call with your new variable.

Because the variable strMessage contains the message text we can now use the variable in place of the text originally entered:

```
Call MsgBox( "Thank you for pressing me" )
```

Becomes

```
Call MsgBox( strMessage)
```

Your code should now look like this:

```
Private Sub cmdPressMe_Click()
Call ThankYouMessage
End Sub

Sub ThankYouMessage()
strMessage = "Thank you for pressing me"
Beep
Call MsgBox(strMessage)
End Sub
```

Session4a

6   Test the command button.

Switch to Form view. When you click the command button you should still hear a beep and see the message displayed in a dialog box proving that your new variable is working properly.

Lesson 4-5: Use the immediate window to view and change variable contents

We've already seen how easy it is to set breakpoints and to step through code using the debug tools.

Programmers often want to examine the contents of different variables at particular points in code execution. The Immediate window lets you do just that. It's hard to exaggerate how useful the Immediate window is when de-bugging code.

1   Set a break point in your code on the Beep command in the ThankYouMessage sub routine.

2   Click the command button on your frmTest form to begin code execution.

The code editor window opens with code execution halted at the Beep command.

```
Private Sub cmdPressMe_Click()
Call ThankYouMessage
End Sub


Private Sub ThankYouMessage()
    strMessage = "Thank you for pressing me"
    Beep
    Call MsgBox(strMessage)
End Sub
```

3   Enable the Immediate Window if it is not already visible.

The immediate window will be at the bottom of the code window if it is enabled. If not select View→Immediate Window from the main menu to make it appear.

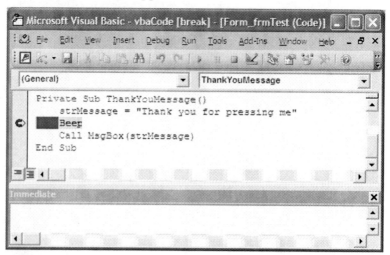

4   Display the contents of the strMessage variable in the immediate window.

Session4b

Type the text *? strMessage* in the immediate window and then press the <Enter> key. The question mark is a throw-back to the very first version of the Basic language and means "Print". You will use the question mark a lot in the immediate window.

The contents of the variable strMessage is displayed.

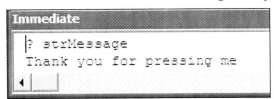

5   Display the literal result of a calculation in the Immediate window.

You can type any arithmetic expression into the immediate window. For example type *? 10/3* and then press the <Enter> key. The answer is displayed.

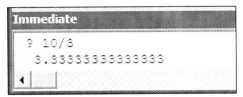

6   Change the value of the strMessage variable using the immediate window.

Sometimes it is useful to change the values of a variable at a break point in your code.

Type *strMessage = "Quite amazing"* in the immediate window followed by the <Enter> key.

7   View the new value of strMessage using an Auto Data Tip.

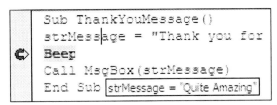

If you hover the mouse cursor over either instance of strMessage within your code an Auto Data Tip will appear showing the current contents of the variable.

8   Click the Continue button [►] on the Debug toolbar to execute the remainder of the code.

The message box is displayed with the new message.

Lesson 4-6: Use the locals window to view and change variable contents

If you thought that the immediate window was amazing you'll find the locals window even more so.

This window allows you to see the values of all currently available variables (variables that are currently available are said to be *in scope*. We'll be learning more about scope in a later lesson).

1   Set a break point in your code on the Beep command in the ThankYouMessage sub routine.

2   Click the command button on your frmTest form to begin code execution.

The code editor window opens with code execution halted at the Beep command.

```
Private Sub cmdPressMe_Click()
Call ThankYouMessage
End Sub


Private Sub ThankYouMessage()
    strMessage = "Thank you for pressing me"
    Beep
    Call MsgBox(strMessage)
End Sub
```

3   Click the Locals Window button ⊞ on the debug toolbar.

The contents of the variable strMessage is displayed within the locals window.

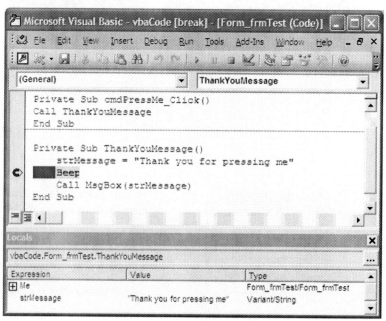

4   Click on the Value "Thank you for pressing me", change the text to "Unbelievable!!" and press the <Enter> key.

Session4b

The strMessage variable now contains a new value.

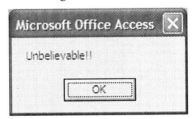

5   Click the Continue Button ➤ on the debug toolbar.

The message box displays the new contents of the variable strMessage.

The Continue Button ➤ is very useful when you are no longer interested in stepping through any more of your code and simply want to resume program execution.

Session 4: Exercise

1   Create a new blank database named *Exercise 4*.

2   Create a new form and save it with the name *frmTest*.

3   Add a command button to the form and set its Caption property to *Log In* with the first letter *(L)* as the hotkey.

4   Because the command button has the caption *Log In* there can only be one possible name for the control in order to observe the *Cradle to the Grave Naming Convention.* Set the *Name* property of the command button to the appropriate value.

When you have finished check that you have correctly set the name and caption of the command button by sliding the page slightly to the left to view the Q4 answer.

5   Go to the event handler for the command button's Click event. Create two variables there called strLogInName and strLogInPassword containing the following data:

strLogInName   David Bowie

strPassword   HunkyDory

6   Add code to the event handler that will put the following dialog on screen by concatenating the text within the two variables.

Only if you are unable to do this check the code listing by sliding the page to the left and viewing the Q6 answer.

7   Set a breakpoint at the *Call MsgBox...* line in your code. Execute your code by clicking the *cmdLogIn* button.

8   Use the Immediate window to change the strName value from *David Bowie* to *Mick Jagger*.

9   Continue code execution and observe the new message that is displayed.

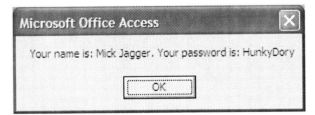

If you had any difficulty with this, slide the page to the left for instructions upon how to progress in the Q9 answer.

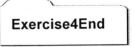

Exercise4End

Session 4: Exercise answers

Q 9	Q 6	Q 4
| To set a break point click in the margin to the left of the code line beginning with **Call MsgBox...**<br><br>Return to the form, enter Form View and then click the command button. Code execution will halt at the break point.<br><br>Bring up the Immediate window by selecting *View→Immediate Window* from the main menu.<br><br>Type in the Immediate Window:<br><br>strLogInName="Mick Jagger" followed by the <Enter> key.<br><br>Continue code execution by<br><br>clicking the *Continue button* on the Debug toolbar. | ```
Private Sub cmdLogIn_Click()
strLogInName = "David Bowie"
strPassword = "HunkyDory"
Call MsgBox("Your name is: " & strLogInName & ". Your password is: " & strPassword)
End Sub
``` | You should have typed **&Log In** as the caption for the command button.<br><br>The command button name should be:<br><br>**cmdLogIn** |
```

Session Five: Professional Grade VBA

> The most important thing I have learned over the years is the difference between taking one's work seriously and taking one's self seriously. The first is imperative, and the second disastrous.
>
> *Dame Margot Fonteyn (1919-1991), British ballet dancer*

In the previous session we covered the bare bones of the VBA language.

Unfortunately the code you have written so far is well below professional standards. It is, however, the type of code that many beginner and self-taught programmers might write.

So what's wrong with the code? You'll find out in this session when we migrate our low-grade code into something a professional would be proud of.

In order to write high quality code there are a few new concepts we need to take on board. You'll learn it all in this session and will then be able to write robust, bug-free, crash-proof code that will be wonderful to work with.

Session Objectives

By the end of this session you will be able to:

- Understand data types
- Understand and implement strong typing
- Understand and implement explicit variable declaration
- Understand arguments
- Understand functions
- Understand ByRef and ByVal argument types
- Set and retrieve form control values from within VBA
- Understand scope
- Implement error handling
- Use the help system and the object browser

Session5

Lesson 5-1: Understand data types

VBA Commonly Used Data Types

Data Type	Value range	Used for
String	64,000 characters	Text.
Currency	Roughly +- 1,000,000,000,000.0000	Precise calculations involving money to four decimal places.
Boolean	True/False	True/False values (as -1 and 0).
Date	January 1st 100 to January 1st 9999	Dates and times accurate to one second.
Double	IEEE 64-bit (8-byte) floating-point numbers.	Very large and very small decimal numbers where absolute precision is not an issue.
Long Integer	32 bit integers from -2,147,483,648 to 2,147,483,647	The preferred data type for all integer values.
Integer	16-bit integers from -32,768 to 32,767	Not generally used. Integer is only included for backward compatibility as Long is faster and more reliable.
Variant	A special type that can contain any kind of data	Many novice programmers use variants for everything!

Copyright (c) 2002-2006 The Smart Method Ltd

VBA Lesser Used Data Types

Data Type	Value range	Used for
Byte	Single unsigned numbers from 0-255	Binary manipulation. Little real-world application within business applications.
Object	32-bit (4-byte) addresses that refer to objects	Object references when the object type is not known (late bound). Largely avoided for the same reason as variants. In most cases Objects should always be strongly typed.
Single	IEEE 32-bit (4-byte) floating-point numbers	Floating point calculations where memory is an issue. Rarely used as memory is not usually an issue with modern hardware.
User Defined	Defined by user	Data types designed by the user often to mimic database records. Rarely used because a better approach would be to use a class (user defined object).

Copyright (c) 2002-2006 The Smart Method Ltd

Up until now we haven't informed VBA about the data type of the variables we're working with. No professional programmer would dream of using variables in this way. By telling VBA that a variable has a data type we can prevent a whole class of bugs that are caused by data type errors. For example, if we try to calculate the sum of two string variables this will only trigger an error if VBA knows that their data type is string.

Before discussing how we strongly type in code let's review the data types that are available and discuss where they might be used.

Session5

String

String variables can contain up to 64,000 characters so are great for storing variables such as names and addresses.

Currency

The currency data type is a *precise* data type. This means that, unlike floating point types, numbers are stored at exactly their value. Always use this data type for money values rather than Doubles.

Boolean

The simple True/False variable. Internally Booleans are implemented as integers that can only have a value of either 0 (for False) or -1 (for True).

Date

Date variables are stored internally as numeric variables with the Date part as the integer and the Time part following the decimal place. The integer part stores the number of days elapsed since December 30th 1899 (negative if before) and the decimal part as the elapsed time during that day since midnight.

For example: 6pm on January 1st 1900 is stored as 1.75 (also see sidebar).

Double

A Double is a floating point number that can be used to store both huge and tiny numbers. For example, the double is able to store a number well in excess of the total number of atoms in the universe.

The problem with the Double type is that not all numbers in a Double's range can be expressed in binary form so many numbers must be stored as approximate values. This approximation often causes rounding errors that are unacceptable in financial systems. Never use this data type for monetary values.

Integer/Long Integer

Integers are a throw-back to earlier versions of VBA. In this version of VBA they are converted (by the compiler) to Long Integers removing any memory saving advantage and making them slower to execute because of the conversion overhead. Always use the Long Integer data type to precisely store whole numbers.

Variant

You created a Variant data type in the last session when the type was not declared. With very few exceptions, Variants should never be used.

Lesson 5-2: Understand and implement strong typing and explicit variable declaration

Weakly typed variables (that will always be of data type Variant) will often result in problems such as "penny rounding" errors in financial calculations. They also introduce the possibility of many potential bugs remaining undetected in your code. For this reason they are never, ever, used by professional programmers.

In the few cases where variants are useful a professional programmer would still strongly type the variable as type *Variant*.

We're going to strongly type the variables created earlier to tell VBA that their data type is string.

We're also going to improve our code yet further by switching on VBA's *explicit variable declaration* option in order to force all future variables to be declared.

1   Open the VBACode.mdb database (if not already open) and open frmTest in Design View.

2   Open the VBA Editor.

3   Edit the code in the ThankYouMessage sub.

In order to demonstrate the benefits of explicit variable declaration we'll introduce a bug. Change the line:

```
Call MsgBox(strMessage)
```

To:

```
Call MsgBox(strMassage)
```

Note the misspelling of *strMassage* in the second case.

4   Execute the buggy code.

Return to Form view and click the cmdPressMe command button. An empty message box is displayed.

This happens because VBA created a new variable called strMassage when it was encountered for the first time. Because this new variable contained no text an empty message box was displayed.

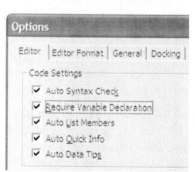

Consider the problems this could cause if you misspelt dblProfitMargin as dblProfitMorgin and then used this value to sell all of your goods at cost price!

It would be a better thing for this type of spelling mistake bug to be trapped as soon as it occurs. We can do this with explicit variable declaration.

5   Switch on explicit variable declaration.

Select Tools→Options from the main menu and then click the Editor tab. Check the *Require Variable Declaration* check box.

Session5

note

You may have noticed that there is also an *Option Compare Database* declaration automatically set by Access.

This dictates the default comparison method to use when string data is compared and can be set to Database, Binary or Text.

The *Option Compare Database* declaration results in string comparisons based upon the sort order determined by the locale ID of the database where the string comparisons occur.

Most Access applications will use this setting as it is the most logical choice.

important

It is possible to declare more than one variable within a single *Dim* statement but this practice is frowned upon by professional programmers.

At first glance you may think that:-

```
Dim strOne,strTwo _
as string
```

Was functionally equivalent to:-

```
Dim strOne as String
Dim strTwo as String
```

The first example would, in fact, declare *strOne* as a Variant and only *strTwo* as a string.

For this reason we have a coding standard that demands that variables be declared individually.

This rule is also included in *Appendix A-The Rules*.

This will add an *Option Explicit* statement at the top of every *future* code module you create. As the module we've been working on already exists we will need to add the statement manually.

6 Add an *Option Explicit* statement at the very top of the code window.

```
Option Explicit

Private Sub cmdPressMe_Click()
    Call ThankYouMessage
End Sub
```

7 Declare and strongly type the *strMessage* variable in the *ThankYouMessage* sub procedure by editing your code to match the following:

```
Option Explicit

Private Sub cmdPressMe_Click()
Call ThankYouMessage
End Sub

Sub ThankYouMessage()
Dim strMessage As String
strMessage = "Thank you for pressing me"
Beep
Call MsgBox(strMassage)
End Sub
```

Note that the spelling mistake of *strMassage* is still present.

8 Execute the code

Return to Form view and click the cmdPressMe command button. The view is switched to the code editor window with the error highlighted:

Click the OK button and correct the error by typing *strMessage* over the misspelt variable.

The code remains frozen with Sub ThankYouMessage() highlighted in yellow.

9 Resume code execution by clicking the Continue button on the VBA Editor toolbar.

The de-bugged code shows the Message Box correctly:

Lesson 5-3: Understand arguments

note

Some programmers prefer the term *Parameter* instead of *Argument*. Both are correct.

An argument is a value that may be passed to a sub or function. Arguments usually modify the behavior of the sub or function in some way.

In this lesson we'll refine our ThankYouMessage sub even further by adding two arguments to it.

1   Open the VBACode.mdb database (if not already open) and open frmTest in Design View.

2   Open the VBA Editor.

Right click on the Command Button and select Build Event from the shortcut menu. The code for the Command Button's Click event is displayed in the code editor.

3   Add an argument to the ThankYouMessage sub.

Edit the code so that it is the same as the following:

```
Private Sub cmdPressMe_Click()

Dim strMessage As String
strMessage = "Thank you for pressing me"

Call ThankYouMessage(strMessage)

End Sub

Sub ThankYouMessage(strMessage As String)

Beep
Call MsgBox(strMessage)

End Sub
```

Consider what is now happening. The strMessage variable is being passed as an argument from the cmdPressMe_Click() event handler to the ThankYouMessage sub.

4   Add a second argument to the ThankYouMessage sub to allow a title to be specified.

Edit the code so that it is the same as the following:

```
Private Sub cmdPressMe_Click()

Dim strMessage As String
Dim strTitle As String

strMessage = "Thank you for pressing me"
strTitle = "Thank You"
Call ThankYouMessage(strMessage, strTitle)

End Sub

Sub ThankYouMessage(strMessage As String, _
                    strTitle As String)

Beep
Call MsgBox(strMessage,,strTitle)
```

Session5a

```
End Sub
```

Passing the arguments is quite straightforward. There are simply two arguments now instead of one.

Note that the MsgBox function has two commas between the *strMessage* and *strTitle* arguments rather than one. This is because the MsgBox function accepts the Title as its third argument, the second argument is optional.

Note also the continuation character (an underscore) after the first argument declaration for the ThankYouMessage sub.

Use continuation characters to break up long lines of code so that they can be viewed within the code editor window without having to use the scrollbars.

5   Test the command button.

Switch to Form View. When you click the command button you should still hear a beep and see the message and title displayed in a dialog box.

This proves that both your arguments are being passed correctly.

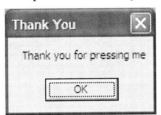

Lesson 5-4: Understand functions

A function is a special type of sub that returns a value. Functions usually (but not always) accept one or more arguments.

In this lesson we'll create a new command button that adds two numbers together and displays the result in a message box using your ThankYouMessage sub procedure.

1 If it is not already open, open the VBACode.mdb spreadsheet and open frmTest in Design View.

2 Add a new command button. Set the *Caption* property to *&Add Two Numbers* and the *Name* property to *cmdAddTwoNumbers*.

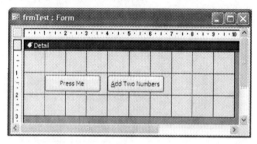

3 Open the command button's Click event handler.

Right click on the *Add Two Numbers* Command Button and select *Build Event* from the shortcut menu and then *Code Builder* from the Choose Builder dialog. The code for the Command Button's Click event is displayed in the code editor.

4 Add the following code to the cmdAddTwoNumbers_click event handler and create your first function: *AddTwoNumbers()* :

```
Private Sub cmdAddTwoNumbers_Click()

Dim dblFirstNumber As Double
Dim dblSecondNumber As Double
Dim dblSumOfNumbers As Double

dblFirstNumber = InputBox("Enter the first number: ")
dblSecondNumber = InputBox("Enter the second number: ")

dblSumOfNumbers = AddTwoNumbers(dblFirstNumber, _
                          dblSecondNumber)

Call ThankYouMessage("The sum of the numbers is: " & _
                   dblSumOfNumbers, _
                   "Result")

End Sub

Function AddTwoNumbers(dblFirstNumber As Double, _
                    dblSecondNumber As Double)

AddTwoNumbers = dblFirstNumber + dblSecondNumber

End Function
```

note

You may wonder why VBA did not report an error when you concatenated a string expression with a double in the line:

```
"The sum of the" & _
"numbers is: " _ &
dblSumOfNumbers
```

It would have been better coding practice to explicitly convert the datatype with the following code:

```
"The sum of the" & _
"numbers is: " _ &
CStr(dblSumOfNumbers)
```

The ability of VBA to perform automatic type conversion (in this case a double to a string) can be useful to beginners but is a thorn in the side of professional programmers who would rather it never happened.

The new versions of stand-alone VB (VB-Net or VB2005) have addressed this problem by allowing programmers to suppress the automatic type conversion behaviour.

Unfortunately it isn't possible to suppress this "feature" in VBA.

Session5b

We have already encountered the MsgBox() VBA function. Now we're encountering the InputBox() function for the first time.

The InputBox function puts up a dialog box on the screen to request input from a user and then returns the value that they type in.

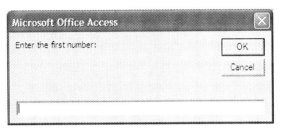

You should have enough understanding from the previous lesson to be able to figure out how most of the rest of the code works.

The only line that may not be intuitive is:

```
AddTwoNumbers = dblFirstNumber + dblSecondNumber
```

In order to tell a function which value it should return, the name of the function (in this case AddTwoNumbers) is stated followed by the assignment operator (=) and the value that you wish to return.

5 **Test the command button.**

Switch to Form view. When you click the command button you should see the first input box displayed. Enter a numeric value and then click the OK button.

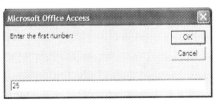

The second input box is displayed. Enter another numeric value and then click the OK button.

The result is then displayed in a message box (using the ThankYouMessage sub procedure).

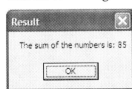

Lesson 5-5: Understand ByRef and ByVal argument types

In the last two lessons you've learned that a sub is used when no return value is required and that a function is simply a sub that returns a value.

In this lesson you'll learn that there is a way to make a function return more than one value, and even a way to return a value from a sub, by passing arguments by *Reference* rather than by *Value*.

There is a crucial difference between passing by reference and by value and this lesson will enable you to decide upon the most appropriate method for your needs.

1   If it is not already open, open the VBACode.mdb spreadsheet and open frmTest in Design View.

2   Add a new command button. Set the *Caption* property to *&By Reference* and the *Name* property to *cmdByReference*.

3   Add another new command button. Set the *Caption* property to *&By Value* and the *Name* property to *cmdByValue*.

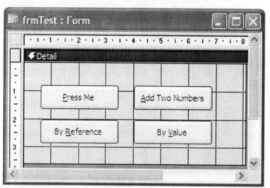

4   Add two new subs to *frmTest* called *ByReference* and *ByValue* with the following code:

```
Sub ByReference(ByRef strMessage As String)
strMessage = "Changed by the ByReference sub"
End Sub

Sub ByValue(ByVal strMessage As String)
strMessage = "Changed by the ByVal sub"
End Sub
```

Note the *ByRef* and *ByVal* prefixes for each argument. The significance of this will become apparent later in the lesson.

5   Add the following code to the Click event handlers for each of the two new command buttons:

```
Private Sub cmdByReference_Click()
Dim strMessage As String
strMessage = "You can change me"

Call ByReference(strMessage)

Call MsgBox("The message is: " & strMessage)
End Sub
```

Session5c

```
Private Sub cmdByValue_Click()
Dim strMessage As String
strMessage = "You can't change me"

Call ByValue(strMessage)

Call MsgBox("The message is: " & strMessage)
End Sub
```

6   Click the cmdByReference command button.

It can be seen that when a variable is passed *By Reference* it is possible for a sub to change the variable's contents.

7   Click the cmdByValue command button.

It can be seen that when a variable is passed *By Value* it is impossible for a sub to change the variable's contents.

8   Delete the cmdByReference and cmdByValue command buttons and associated code.

When to pass variables By Reference

Some programmers would argue that you should never pass a variable by reference because it violates the principle of encapsulation and introduces a source of potential bugs into your code.

In VBA all arguments are passed by reference as the default (you don't even have to use the ByRef keyword). Microsoft have probably made this decision because passing arguments by reference is slightly faster than by value as the contents of the variable don't have to be duplicated in memory.

In our own code we generally side with the first school of thought and declare all arguments ByVal but we do use ByRef as a quick and convenient way of returning multiple values from functions (or subs).

Lesson 5-6: Set and retrieve form control values from within VBA

Appreciate that all form controls are objects with Properties, Methods and Events. We are going to refine frmTest so that the user can enter the numbers to be added into text boxes on the form. We can then pick up the values by inspecting the *Value* property of each *Text Box* object and will then display the result in a *Text Box* control on the same form.

1   Add three text box controls and three label controls to the form so that it looks like this:

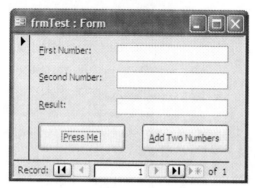

2   Name the three Text Box controls txtFirstNumber, txtSecondNumber and txtResult.

3   Change the appearance of the txtResult text box by setting the following properties:

Make sure you are in Design View before changing the properties otherwise you won't see any effect until the form is closed, saved and re-opened. Note also that, due to a bug in Access, the *Border Color* property must be set first (see sidebar).

Property	Value	
Border Color	8421504 (Gray)	This color works well for the sunken border.
Border Style	Solid	The sunken effect needs a border.
Locked	Yes	Stops the user typing into the control.
Enabled	No	Stops the control having focus.
Tab stop	No	Takes the control out of the tab order.
Back Style	Transparent	Makes the inside color of the control the same as the form.
Special Effect	Sunken	Makes the control appear sunken.

Session5c

tip

The line
`Me.txtFirstNumber.Value`
returns the *Value* property of the text box named *txtFirstNumber* on the current form.

Even though the *Me* keyword is optional it is extremely useful as typing Me followed by a dot will display all objects relevant to **this form**.

You may, of course, want to also access properties from controls on other forms when the Me keyword would not be appropriate. We'll discover how to do this in a future session.

Important

Default properties

VBA has a very confusing "feature" in that every control has a default property.

Me.txtResult.Value

and

Me.txtResult

...are functionally equivalent because *Value* is the default property of an Access *Text Box* control.

The default property feature has (thankfully) been removed from the latest versions of stand-alone VB (VB.Net and VB 2005) showing that Microsoft also agree that it isn't the best feature in the world.

Never use default properties in your VBA code as they make the code less readable and more prone to error (as the actual property being manipulated must remain in the programmer's memory).

This information is provided so that you will understand code samples and code within existing applications as many non-professional programmers are extremely fond of using default properties.

The text box now has an appearance that intuitively tells the user that it is a read-only control.

Another commonly used style for read-only text boxes is the *Flat* effect. Use whichever you like the look of best.

Result:

4 Open the VBA Editor.

Right click on the *cmdAddTwoNumbers* Command Button and select *Build Event* from the shortcut menu (select Code Builder from the Choose Builder dialog if it appears). The code for the Command Button's Click event is displayed in the code editor.

5 Modify the code so that the input values are taken from the relevant Text Box's Value property and written to the txtResult control's Value property.

Note the use of dot notation to reference each object's properties.

```
Private Sub cmdAddTwoNumbers_Click()

Dim dblFirstNumber As Double
Dim dblSecondNumber As Double
Dim dblSumOfNumbers As Double

dblFirstNumber = Me.txtFirstNumber.Value
dblSecondNumber = Me.txtSecondNumber.Value

dblSumOfNumbers = AddTwoNumbers(dblFirstNumber, _
                                dblSecondNumber)

Me.txtResult.Value = dblSumOfNumbers

End Sub
```

6 Test the command button.

Switch to Form view. Enter two numeric values into the text boxes and then click the *Add Two Numbers* command button.

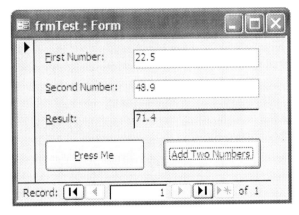

Lesson 5-7: Understand scope

What is scope?

Every variable that you declare has scope.

The word: *visibility* is often used in place of *scope* and is a more intuitive word for describing the concept.

There are three possible scopes for a variable:

Local

Some programmers insist that this is the only type of variable that should ever be declared (though in reality life would be very difficult without the use of Module scoped variables).

A local variable is only available within the sub or function in which it is declared.

Every variable declared with a Dim statement within a sub or function has local visibility.

Module (or Private)

Module level variables have many indispensable uses but should be used sparingly and with caution. Module level variables are visible within the code module in which they are declared. There's a code module behind every form and report and you can also create modules that are not associated with any form or report.

Every variable declared with a Dim statement at the top of a module (just after the Option Explicit statement) will have module visibility.

Good naming convention requires that module level variables be prefixed with a lowercase letter *m*, for example *mstrFormMode*. (This rule and others are included in *Appendix A – The Rules*).

Public

Many programmers believe that the use of Public variables should never be tolerated. They have the ability to completely destroy the integrity of your application and to make it almost impossible to debug. We'd agree with this view.

Public variables shouldn't be confused with public constants which are extremely useful. In a later lesson we'll create a public constant to store the name of the application so that changing it in one place will propagate the change throughout the application.

For now it is enough to remember that the use of Public variables is almost always a bad idea.

1   Declare a module-level (Private) variable

Add the following code to the very top of the form module (just under Option Explicit.

```
Dim mlngCounter As Long
```

note

Why Module level variables can be dangerous

Many beginner or self-taught programmers will inappropriately use a module level variable instead of sub and function arguments. This approach results in very buggy code.

For example: a novice programmer might think that instead of having the argument *strMessage as String* passed into the *ThankYouMessage* sub it would be easier to declare a module-level variable called *mstrMessage*.

The *mstrMessage* variable would then be set before calling *ThankYouMessage* with no arguments like this:

```
mstrMessage = "Hello"
Call ThankYouMessage
```

This approach introduces the possibility of a new class of bugs as the contents of mstrMessage can easily be corrupted.

Session5d

Because the variable is declared outside any sub it is visible throughout this module (but nowhere else).

2   Add code to update the counter every time a command button is clicked.

Add the following code to each command button's event handler:

```
mlngCounter = mlngCounter + 1
Me.Caption = "You have now clicked: " & _
mlngCounter & " times this session"
```

The code will update the module-level variable to keep a running total of the number of times either command button has been clicked since the form was opened. The total number of clicks will then be displayed in the caption of the form.

3   Test your form.

Code listing

```
Option Explicit
Dim mlngCounter As Long

Private Sub cmdAddTwoNumbers_Click()
Dim dblFirstNumber As Double
Dim dblSecondNumber As Double
Dim dblSumOfNumbers As Double
Dim strSumOfNumbers As String

mlngCounter = mlngCounter + 1
Me.Caption = "You have now clicked: " & mlngCounter & "
times this session"

dblFirstNumber = Me.txtFirstNumber.Value
dblSecondNumber = Me.txtSecondNumber.Value
dblSumOfNumbers = AddTwoNumbers(dblFirstNumber,
dblSecondNumber)

strSumOfNumbers = CStr(dblSumOfNumbers)
lblResult.Caption = strSumOfNumbers

End Sub

Private Sub cmdPressMe_Click()

Dim strMessage As String
Dim strTitle As String

mlngCounter = mlngCounter + 1

Me.Caption = "You have now clicked: " & mlngCounter & "
times this session"
strMessage = "Thank you for pressing me"
strTitle = "Thank you"
Call ThankYouMessage(strMessage, strTitle)

End Sub
```

note

There's nothing more unprofessional (from a client's perspective) than an application that frequently crashes.

One of our most important quality standards *(stated in Appendix A – The Rules)* states that:

"Error Handling must be implemented in every sub and function without exception".

Programmers often argue that some code is so simple that it can never fail so does not need error handling. While this may be true in some cases there's nothing wrong with a catch-all approach. If absolutely every sub has error handling code you cannot possibly confront your user with a confidence-sapping runtime error.

When you take this approach it is comforting to find that those bullet-proof subs that couldn't possible fail often do, but when they do the error is always elegantly handled.

Lesson 5-8: Implement error handling

The code that has been written so far has no error handling. This means that when something goes wrong the program "crashes" causing the default error handler to display.

Professional code always includes custom error handling in every sub and function (see sidebar) so that you are in control when something goes wrong. We're now going to add error handling to bring the code to a level that a professional programmer would be proud of.

1   If it is not already open, open the VBACode.mdb spreadsheet and open frmTest in Design View.

2   Enter some text into one of the text boxes instead of a number and then click the Add Two Numbers command button.

A run-time error dialog appears.

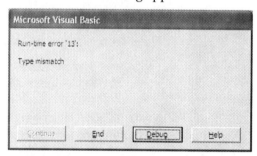

The error appears because Error Handling has not been implemented resulting in the program code crashing.

3   Click the End button, Open the VBA Editor and navigate to the cmdAddTwoNumbers command button's Click event handler.

4   Add error handling code to the cmdAddTwoNumbers command button's Click event handler.

Modify the code as follows (new error handling code is shown boldfaced):

```
Private Sub cmdAddTwoNumbers_Click()

On Error GoTo ErrorHandler

Dim dblFirstNumber As Double
Dim dblSecondNumber As Double
Dim dblSumOfNumbers As Double

mlngCounter = mlngCounter + 1

(Central section of code not shown)

Me.txtResult.Value = dblSumOfNumbers

CleanUpAndExit:
Exit Sub
```

tip

Always use the labels ErrorHandler: and CleanUpAndExit: in every function and sub routine.

There's no reason to give a custom name to every label even though you'll see later that wizard-generated code does this.

Using the same error handler labels keeps your code consistent and improves productivity as you can cut and paste error handling code from one sub to another.

Session5e

note

The logic behind using a *Resume* statement to exit an error handler is that a block of *cleanup code* can be inserted in one place within the sub. In later lessons we'll explore the concept of *cleanup code* in more detail.

A very old and very wise programming standard insists that there should be only one exit from a sub and this rule is included in *Appendix A – The Rules*.

In this simple sub, and in all code encountered so far, no cleanup code is required.

Later when we work with object variables (that must be destroyed at the end of the sub) you will see the logic in putting cleanup code in one place.

note

vbCrLf is one of VBA's built-in constants that contains a concatenated carriage return and line feed character to move to the next line.

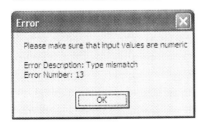

```
ErrorHandler:

Call MsgBox("Please ensure that input values are
numeric")
Resume CleanUpAndExit
```

End Sub

Let's discuss the error handling code.

```
On Error GoTo ErrorHandler
```

The very first line of the code tells VBA that if an error occurs it must execute the code that begins after the label `ErrorHandler:`

```
CleanUpAndExit:
Exit Sub
```

The `CleanUpAndExit` label identifies the beginning of code that must execute before exiting the sub. In a future session we'll discuss the concept of clean up code. Even though no clean up code is required in this simple sub, having a single exit point in absolutely every sub is a great habit to get into. Multiple exit points are a major cause of bugs in novice code.

The `Exit Sub` statement usually immediately precedes the `ErrorHandler:` label and is the single exit point of the sub. Note that after the error message is displayed code execution continues at the `CleanUpAndExit:` label (branched to with the `Resume CleanUpAndExit` statement) to observe the single exit rule.

5 Test your code.

Switch to Form View. Enter some invalid (non numeric) text into one of the boxes and then click the *Add Two Numbers* command button. This time the error is gracefully handled and a user-friendly message box is displayed.

6 Improve the error handling code by giving the user more information.

In this simple function there's very little that can go wrong. If there's an error we're pretty certain that the user has entered invalid values. Many functions aren't quite as simple and have potential for many different errors.

To provide better feedback we use the error object (Err). The Error object has *Number* and *Description* properties containing more information about the last encountered error.

Modify the error handler code as follows:

```
ErrorHandler:
Call MsgBox("Please ensure that input values are
numeric" & vbCrLf & _
vbCrLf & _
"Error Description: " & Err.Description & vbCrLf & _
"Error Number: " & Err.Number, , "Error")
Resume CleanUpAndExit
```

7 Test your code.

This time an even better error dialog appears:

Lesson 5-9: Use the help system and the object browser

The Visual Basic help system can provide all of the information you need about both the Visual Basic programming language and the Access object model. This session will teach you how to quickly find help on any topic.

Getting help using the Visual Basic help system

1   Open the code editor and click on the object name *Err* in the error handler for the cmdAddTwoNumbers event handler.

```
Err.Description
```

2   Press the F1 key.

The Help system starts and displays information about the Error object. Links are also provided to list the object's properties and methods.

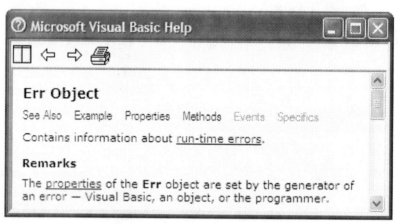

Getting help using the Object Browser

The object browser provides a quick reference to all of the objects in the Access object model. Each object's *Properties, Methods* and *Events* are also documented.

1   Open the VBA editor.

2   Open the object browser by either pressing the <F2> key, by selecting View→Object Browser from the menu, or by clicking the Object Browser button 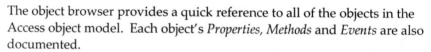 on the standard toolbar.

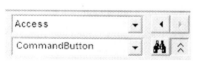

3   Select *Access* from the drop down list in the top left corner of the Object Browser.

4   Type *CommandButton* (no spaces) in the search box beneath the drop down list.

5   Click the Search button 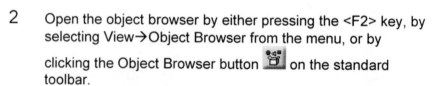.

Session5f

note

The terminology *Class* and *Object* refer to almost the same thing.

A Class is the actual definition of the object. Think of it as the mould from which all new objects are made.

One Class can be used to create any number of Objects.

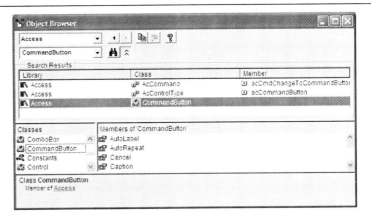

The Search Results pane shows the objects found with the best guesses at the top.

You can click on any of the objects in Search results (or select directly in the Classes pane) to see all properties, methods and events of the chosen object type.

6   Select the *Command Button* object in the top pane and browse all of its Properties, Methods and Events.

Properties are marked with the 📷 icon, Methods with the ◈ icon and Events with the 𝄃 icon.

7   Obtain detailed help on the Command Button's *Click* event.

Scroll down the list of Properties, Methods and Events until you find the Click event.

With the Click event selected click the yellow question mark icon ⍰ at the top of the dialog.

The help system displays detailed help for the Command Button's Click event.

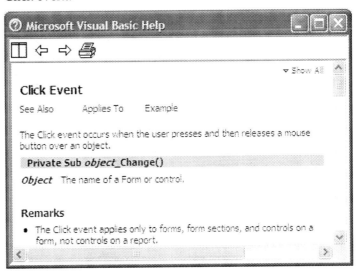

Session 5: Exercise

1 Which data type is appropriate to store the following information?

Purpose

A number used to store a person's age.	☐ Long Integer	☐ Integer	☐ Double
Text that will contain an Employee's last name.	☐ Variant	☐ String	☐ Double
The unit price of items for sale.	☐ Double	☐ Long Integer	☐ Currency
An Employee's date of birth.	☐ Variant	☐ Date	☐ String
The average purchase price of an item to six decimal places.	☐ Long integer	☐ Currency	☐ Double
Whether a client is active or not.	☐ Integer	☐ Variant	☐ Boolean

If you are having difficulty choosing the correct data type complete as many as you are sure of and then slide the page slightly to the left to view the Q1 help and answers.

2 Create a new blank database named *Exercise5*.

3 Create a new form called *frmTest*.

4 Add three text box controls to the form (this will also automatically add three label controls) and a command button. Set the *Caption* property of the labels to *First Name, Last Name* and *Full Name* and the *Caption* property of the command button to *Calculate Full Name*.

5 The *Cradle to the Grave Naming Convention* requires that the names of the captions will dictate the name properties of the three Text Box form controls and Command Button control. Name them correctly.

The correct names for the controls can be viewed by sliding the page to the left and viewing the Q5 answers.

6 Add code to the *cmdCalculateFullName* command button's *Click* event. The code needs to take the two values in the *txtFirstName* and *txtLastName* text boxes, concatenate them with a space between, and then put the result into the *txtFullName* text box.

If you have difficulties coding the event handler slide the page to view the Q6 help.

7 Test your form.

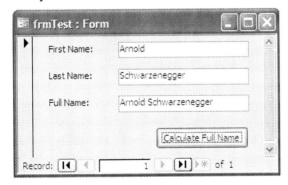

Exercise5

Session 5: Exercise answers

Q 6	Q 5	Q 1

This can be coded in a single line:
 	
```Private Sub cmdCalculateFullName_Click()```
 ```txtFullName.Value = Me.txtFirstName.Value & " " & Me.txtLastName.Value```
 ```End Sub```
	The correct names for the controls can only be:
	
	txtFirstName
	
	txtLastName
	
	txtFullName
	
	cmdCalculateFullName
		A person's age will be a whole number so needs to be stored as an integer. Only long integers are commonly used in contemporary VBA programming (the short integer is only used for backward compatibility). The correct answer is thus: Long Integer.
		
		An Employee's last name should be stored in a String variable.
		
		Unit price (and all monetary values) should always be stored in the precise *Currency* data type and never in the approximate *Double* data type.
		
		Date of Birth can only be sensibly be stored in a Date data type.
		
		Average Purchase Price to six decimal places may, at first glance, appear to be suited to the Currency data type. Because the Currency type only stores up to four decimal places this isn't possible so you should use the Double data type.
		
		Whether a client is active or not can only be True or False so is best suited to a Boolean data type.

Session Six: Improving Wizard-Generated Code

There are two ways to generate Access VBA code automatically. You can convert any Access macro into VBA code or allow one of the Wizards to generate code for you.

Code generated by macros or wizards provides a useful insight into the correct properties, methods and events needed to implement a lot of commonly required features. More importantly, the Access experts who wrote the wizards have vast experience in the best way of reliably implementing this functionality.

While wizard code is a great way to learn about VBA programming and the Access object model it often needs refining to provide exactly what you need and you will often need to ignore Tolkien's advice and improve their code.

This session will empower you to completely understand the code the wizards have generated and even to improve it a little.

Session Objectives

By the end of this session you will be able to:

- Improve wizard generated error handling
- Understand the DoCmd object and some of its methods
- Replace standard warnings and error messages with custom dialogs
- Understand all wizard code previously generated
- Modify and improve wizard code functionality
- Correctly name controls

Session6

Lesson 6-1: Understand and improve the command button wizard's error handling code

note

The logic behind using a *Resume* statement to exit an error handler is that a block of *cleanup code* can be inserted in one place within the sub. In later lessons we'll explore the concept of *cleanup code* in more detail.

A very old and very wise programming standard insists that there should be only one exit from a sub and this rule is included in *Appendix A – The Rules*.

In this simple sub, and in all code encountered so far, no cleanup code is required.

Later when we work with object variables (that must be destroyed at the end of the sub) you will see the logic in putting cleanup code in one place.

1   Open the FilmLibrary.MDB database.

2   Open the frmFilm form in Design View.

3   Open the VBA Editor and navigate to the cmdDelete_Click event handler.

The code for the Command Button's Click event is displayed in the code editor.

```
Private Sub cmdDelete_Click()

On Error GoTo Err_cmdDelete_Click

DoCmd.DoMenuItem acFormBar, acEditMenu, 8, ,acMenuVer70
DoCmd.DoMenuItem acFormBar, acEditMenu, 6, ,acMenuVer70

Exit_cmdDelete_Click:
    Exit Sub

Err_cmdDelete_Click:
    MsgBox Err.Description
    Resume Exit_cmdDelete_Click

End Sub
```

4   Understand and improve the error handling portion of the code.

You should now understand most of the error handling code in the cmdDelete command button's Click event handler.

Unlike our earlier hand-crafted code the Wizard has used the label Err_cmdDelete_Click for the Error Handler label instead of our preferred generic *ErrorHandler* label but we can live with that. Don't do this in your own code though as it will make the error handling code less easy to cut and paste between subs.

Note that the wizard is observing the one-exit rule by using a Resume statement to return execution at the Exit_cmdDelete_Click: label before exiting. While this adds nothing to the sub in its present form we'll add extra functionality to this sub later and you'll then appreciate the value of a single exit point.

5   Improve the Error Message provided to the user.

The Wizard has provided a very basic error message to the user. It simply provides the *Description* property of the *Err* object in a message box. If the user cancels the delete operation the following dialog is displayed:

Session6

This isn't very intuitive. Let's provide more information to the user by modifying the code as follows:

```
Private Sub cmdDelete_Click()

On Error GoTo Err_cmdDelete_Click

DoCmd.DoMenuItem acFormBar, acEditMenu, 8, ,acMenuVer70
DoCmd.DoMenuItem acFormBar, acEditMenu, 6, ,acMenuVer70

Exit_cmdDelete_Click:
Exit Sub

Err_cmdDelete_Click:

    Call MsgBox("The record was not deleted" & vbCrLf & _
    vbCrLf & _
    "Description: " & Err.Description & vbCrLf & _
    "Error Number: " & Err.Number, , _
"Error Deleting Record")

Resume Exit_cmdDelete_Click

End Sub
```

6   Test the new error handler

Open the frmFilm form in form view.

This time a much more professional and understandable error dialog appears:

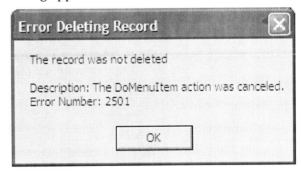

Lesson 6-2: Understand the DoCmd object and it's DoMenuItem method

In this lesson we discover a major flaw in the Command Button's code generator for the Delete action. Believe it or not the Wizard is generating Access Version 95 compatible code and is using coding practices that Microsoft has been advising against since 1997!

Microsoft's help for the DoMenuItem method of the DoCmd object states:

"In Microsoft Access 97, the DoMenuItem method was replaced by the RunCommand method. The DoMenuItem method is included in this version of Microsoft Access only for compatibility with previous versions".

Because the Wizard is using the old *DoMenuItem* method we'll figure out how it is working before replacing it with the recommended *RunCommand* method.

1   Open the frmFilm form in Design View.

2   Open the VBA Editor and inspect the code for the cmdDelete Command Button's *Click* event.

```
Private Sub cmdDelete_Click()

On Error GoTo Err_cmdDelete_Click

DoCmd.DoMenuItem acFormBar, acEditMenu, 8, ,acMenuVer70
DoCmd.DoMenuItem acFormBar, acEditMenu, 6, ,acMenuVer70

Exit_cmdDelete_Click:
Exit Sub
```

(Error handling code not shown)

3   Understand the DoCmd object.

Apart from the error handling code there are only two lines of code in this event handler.

```
DoCmd.DoMenuItem acFormBar, acEditMenu, 8, ,acMenuVer70
DoCmd.DoMenuItem acFormBar, acEditMenu, 6, ,acMenuVer70
```

The first keyword in each case is *DoCmd*. DoCmd is one of the most important objects in the VBA object model and is remarkable in that it has no events or properties but about fifty methods. Browse them using the object browser.

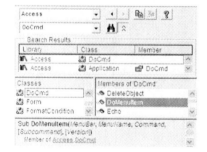

You'll immediately recognise many of DoCmd's methods which echo many of Access's interactive functions but let's focus on the *DoMenuItem* method (which, as discussed, is now officially obsolete)!

4   Understand the DoCmd object's DoMenuItem method parameters.

The bottom line of the Object Browser displays the prototype for the DoMenuItem method:

```
Sub DoMenuItem(MenuBar, MenuName, Command,
[Subcommand], [Version])
```

Session6a

This reveals that the DoMenuItem method has five possible arguments. Those shown in square brackets are optional and the others are mandatory.

Clicking the yellow question mark [?] icon reveals the purpose of each parameter (See sidebar).

5 Understand the MenuBar parameter.

```
DoCmd.DoMenuItem acFormBar, acEditMenu, 8, ,acMenuVer70
DoCmd.DoMenuItem acFormBar, acEditMenu, 6, ,acMenuVer70
```

The first parameter is *acFormBar*. This is a VBA constant (just like vbCrLf). It contains a "magic number" that tells the sub to execute a command contained on the *Form* toolbar.

6 Understand the MenuName parameter.

```
DoCmd.DoMenuItem acFormBar, acEditMenu, 8, ,acMenuVer70
DoCmd.DoMenuItem acFormBar, acEditMenu, 6, ,acMenuVer70
```

In exactly the same way as the MenuBar parameter the MenuName parameter has been set to the constant *acEditMenu* to indicate that the command to be executed is contained in the Edit Menu.

7 Understand the Command parameter.

```
DoCmd.DoMenuItem acFormBar, acEditMenu, 8, ,acMenuVer70
DoCmd.DoMenuItem acFormBar, acEditMenu, 6, ,acMenuVer70
```

There's no constant to make the Command parameter more readable. It is simply the item on the Edit Menu of the Form toolbar where the first item is zero.

So why is the wizard executing Menu item 8 (*Delete* in Access 2003) followed by Menu item 6 (*Paste as Hyperlink* in Access 2003)? The answer is that the numbers relate to Access 95 menu items when there were different items on the Edit menu!

If you are thinking that this is ridiculous, requiring you to have a spare copy of Access 95 running on another machine to even understand it, then you are right!

This poor readability is a compelling reason to take Microsoft's advice and avoid using the obsolete *DoMenuItem* method in your own code.

8 Understand the Version parameter.

The Version parameter reveals the root problem with readability of the code. It has been set to the constant acMenuVer70 meaning that the menu items above relate to their positions in the Access 95 menu system. The constant is so named because Access 95's full name was *Access for Windows 95 Version 7*.

Why not an *acMenuVer2003* constant? A good question but the answer is that it simply doesn't exist, nor do constants for versions 97, 2000 or 2002. It really is an obsolete method, and that's probably a good thing!

DoMenuItem Method

See Also   Applies To
Example

Displays the appropriate menu or toolbar command for Microsoft Access.

expression.DoMenuItem
(*MenuBar, MenuName, Command, Subcommand, Version*)

expression Required. An expression that returns one of the objects in the Applies To list.

MenuBar Required **Variant**. Use the intrinsic constant **acFormBar** for the menu bar in Form view. For other views, use the number of the view in the menu bar argument list, as shown in the Macro window in previous versions of Microsoft Access (count down the list, starting from 0).

MenuName Required **Variant**. You can use one of the following **intrinsic constants**.

Command Required **Variant**. You can use one of the following **intrinsic constants**.

Subcommand Optional **Variant**. You can use one of the following **intrinsic constants**.

Version Optional **Variant**. Use the intrinsic constant **acMenuVer70** for code written for Microsoft Access 95 databases

---

Lesson 6-3: Implement the DoCmd object's RunCommand method

As discussed in the previous lesson the Command Button wizard sometimes uses the obsolete *DoMenuItem* method that is included only for backward compatibility with Access 95.

In this lesson we'll update the code to substitute Microsoft's recommended *RunCommand* method.

1   Open the frmFilm form in Design View.

2   Open the VBA Editor and inspect the code for the cmdDelete Command Button's Click event handler.

```
Private Sub cmdDelete_Click()

On Error GoTo Err_cmdDelete_Click

DoCmd.DoMenuItem acFormBar, acEditMenu, 8, ,acMenuVer70
DoCmd.DoMenuItem acFormBar, acEditMenu, 6, ,acMenuVer70

Exit_cmdDelete_Click:
Exit Sub
```

(Error handling code not shown)

3   Modify the code so that it uses the RunCommand method as follows:

```
Private Sub cmdDelete_Click()

On Error GoTo Err_cmdDelete_Click

Call DoCmd.RunCommand(acCmdDeleteRecord)

Exit_cmdDelete_Click:
Exit Sub

Err_cmdDelete_Click:

  Call MsgBox("The record was not deleted" & vbCrLf & _
  vbCrLf & _
  "Description: " & Err.Description & vbCrLf & _
  "Error Number: " & Err.Number, , _
  "Error Deleting Record")
  Resume Exit_cmdDelete_Click
End Sub
```

4   Test the new method call's Delete functionality.

Open the frmFilm form in form view, add a test record, navigate to the test record and click the Delete button.

The Delete dialog appears.

Session6a

5 Click the Yes button.

The record is deleted.

6 Test the new method call's Delete functionality when deletion of a record is cancelled.

Navigate to any record and click the Delete button.

The Delete dialog appears.

Click the No button.

The Error Handler displays a message informing the user that the delete action did not complete.

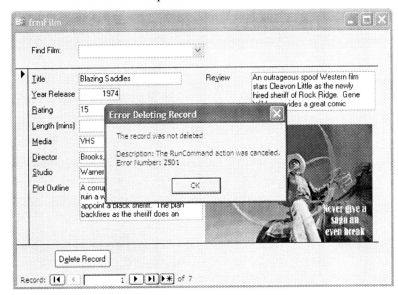

The delete record button is a lot better than it was but perhaps the dialog warning the user about cascading deletes is a little alarming. It would be better to provide a more user-friendly dialog. We'll do that in the next lesson.

Lesson 6-4: Replace standard warnings and error messages with custom dialogs

If this application were only intended for use in a single company environment with appropriate staff training users could accept the rather user-unfriendly error messages that result when a film record is deleted.

For commercial mass-market applications the standard Access dialogs really won't do. We'd like a simple error message that any user will be able to understand without reading a manual.

1   Open the frmFilm form in Design View.

2   Open the VBA Editor and inspect the code for the cmdDelete Command Button's Click event handler.

```
Private Sub cmdDelete_Click()

On Error GoTo Err_cmdDelete_Click

Call DoCmd.RunCommand(acCmdDeleteRecord)

Exit_cmdDelete_Click:
Exit Sub

Err_cmdDelete_Click:

  Call MsgBox("The record was not deleted" & vbCrLf & _
  vbCrLf & _
  "Description: " & Err.Description & vbCrLf & _
  "Error Number: " & Err.Number, , _
"Error Deleting Record")
Resume Exit_cmdDelete_Click
End Sub
```

The problem is caused because the line:

```
Call DoCmd.RunCommand(acCmdDeleteRecord)
```

... displays the Access default dialog.

3   Suppress the standard Access warning dialog using the DoCmd object's SetWarnings method.

Modify the code as follows:

```
Call DoCmd.SetWarnings(False)
Call DoCmd.RunCommand(acCmdDeleteRecord)
Call DoCmd.SetWarnings(True)
```

The deletion will now occur without any warning at all. This is nearer to what we want but we'd still like to give the user the opportunity to cancel the deletion if the delete button is clicked by mistake.

4   Add a custom dialog to allow the user to cancel deletion of a record.

Modify the code as follows:

note

Bit masks

You may wonder why you are able to add the *vbQuestion* and *vbYesNo* constants together to provide a single argument that will result in a Yes/No message box showing a Question icon.

The answer is that these are special types of constants called bit masks.

Without dwelling upon the science behind bit masks it is sufficient to say that they are constants that can be added together to test for multiple conditions.

```
Dim mbxResponse As VbMsgBoxResult

mbxResponse = MsgBox( _
"Are you sure you want to delete this record?", _
vbQuestion + vbYesNo)

If mbxResponse = vbYes Then
    Call DoCmd.SetWarnings(False)
    Call DoCmd.RunCommand(acCmdDeleteRecord)
    Call DoCmd.SetWarnings(True)
Else
    Call MsgBox("The record was not deleted")
End If
```

5   Make the error handling code more robust.

There is a major potential bug within the code as it stands at present. The SetWarnings method will switch off standard Access warnings until Access is closed down so it is essential that we aways switch it back on again. This is done with the line:

```
Call DoCmd.SetWarnings(True)
```

... but consider the case when the deletion fails and the error handler is invoked. In this case execution will branch to the error handler and there will be no more standard warnings during this Access session. This could be potentially disasterous. Because there is only one exit to this sub we can simply add another precautionary *Call DoCmd.SetWarnings(True)* at the single exit point (Exit_cmdDelete_Click:)

Modify the code as follows:

```
Private Sub cmdDelete_Click()
On Error GoTo Err_cmdDelete_Click
Dim mbxResponse As VbMsgBoxResult
mbxResponse = MsgBox( _
"Are you sure you want to delete this record?", _
vbQuestion + vbYesNo)

If mbxResponse = vbYes Then
    Call DoCmd.SetWarnings(False)
    Call DoCmd.RunCommand(acCmdDeleteRecord)
    Call DoCmd.SetWarnings(True)
Else
    Call MsgBox("The record was not deleted")
End If

Exit_cmdDelete_Click:
Call DoCmd.SetWarnings(True)
Exit Sub

Err_cmdDelete_Click:

  Call MsgBox("The record was not deleted" & vbCrLf & _
  vbCrLf & _
  "Description: " & Err.Description & vbCrLf & _
  "Error Number: " & Err.Number, , _
"Error Deleting Record")
Resume Exit_cmdDelete_Click
End Sub
```

Lesson 6-5: Understand the combo box wizard code

note

Early and late binding

The wizard has produced poor quality code by declaring the recordset as simply Object. This type of declaration is called *late binding*.

The Object data type is a little like a variant for objects. It is an object variable that does not know what sort of object it references.

A higher quality approach would be to declare it as follows:-

```
Dim rs as DAO.Recordset
```

This type of declaration is called *early-binding*.

An early bound object runs faster as it does not have to be created at runtime and is easier to work with because all of the properties and methods will appear as an IntelliSense pop-up list.

1   Open the frmFilm form in Design View.

2   Open the VBA Editor and inspect the code for the Find Film combo box's AfterUpdate event.

```
Private Sub Combo21_AfterUpdate()

' Find the record that matches the control.
Dim rs As Object

Set rs = Me.Recordset.Clone
rs.FindFirst "[FilmID] = " & Str(Nz(Me![Combo21], 0))

If Not rs.EOF Then Me.Bookmark = rs.Bookmark

End Sub
```

If your code doesn't look like the above it is probably because you didn't select the FilmID field when you created the combo box using the wizard. If this is the case re-create it before continuing.

3   Understanding the Recordset object.

You already appreciate that every form and report has an SQL query underpinning it. You also know that the SQL query is executed against the database (tables) and returns data. This data is returned in an object called a *Recordset*.

4   View the form's Recordset.

Right-click in the top left corner of the form while in Design View and choose Properties from the shortcut menu to bring up the Form Properties dialog.

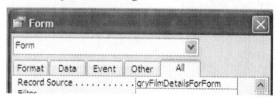

The Form's RecordSource property indicates that this form's recordset is the result of executing the query qryFilmDetailsForForm, the query that we stated when the wizard created the form.

When you click into the RecordSource property a small button with three dots appears next to qryFilmDetailsForForm.

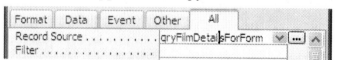

Click the button. The familiar query designer appears.

5   Execute the query to view the recordset that underpins this form.

Click the Run button ![run] on the query design toolbar. The recordset that underpins the form is displayed:

note

The sample code shows the combo box as being named Combo21. It is quite likely that your code will show it with a different name such as Combo23.

The difference is caused by the Wizard naming controls with an arbitrary number since the control name's only requirement is to be unique within the application.

It would be better to rename the control correctly as *cboFindFilm* but to change both the name of the control and code references to it isn't really worth the effort.

Session6b

note

The clone method

Variables that point to objects are a little different to regular variables.

Because it takes a lot of memory to make a copy of a recordset the default behaviour of object variables is to establish a reference to the existing copy of an object.

The code:-

```
Set rs = Me.Recordset
```

Would merely create a pointer to the existing recordset underpinning the form while :-

```
Set rs = _
Me.recordset.clone
```

Will actually make a new copy of the recordset.

Making a copy is vital as otherwise the FindFirst action would corrupt the record currently displayed on the form even if the relevant FilmID was not found.

note

The bookmark property

Every Recordset object has a *bookmark* property.

The bookmark property is used for two purposes:-

1/ To retrieve the bookmark property from the form's current record (the record that is currently being displayed).

2/ To set the form's Current Record in order to display the record of the programmer's choice.

The combo box's *AfterUpdate* event handler retrieves the bookmark property from the cloned recordset (rs.bookmark) and sets the bookmark property of the form's recordset object to match (Me.Recordset.bookmark).

FilmID	Title	Year Released	Rating
1	It's A Wonderful Life	1947	U
2	Casablanca	1942	U
3	Gone With The Wind	1939	PG
4	Blazing Saddles	1974	15
5	Interview With The Vampire	1994	18
6	Get Carter	2000	15
7	Get Carter	1971	18
*	(AutoNumber)		

qryFilmDetailsForForm : Query Builder

The Recordset object is a little like an Excel spreadsheet and contains a column for every field in the query result and a row for every record. The Recordset object has a full complement of methods as well as data.

6 **Understand the Recordset object's Clone method.**

The Clone method makes an exact copy of a recordset.

```
Dim rs As Object
Set rs = Me.Recordset.Clone
```

The above code declares a variable called *rs* of type *Object* and then places into it an exact copy of the Recordset object that underpins this form. See the *clone method* sidebar for more details.

7 **Understand the Recordset object's *FindFirst* method.**

The FindFirst method accepts an SQL WHERE clause as a parameter and uses it to position a pointer (called a bookmark) to the first record matching the WHERE clause in the recordset.

The code takes the default value of the Combo box (the primary key field) and converts it to a string using the *Str* function. The *Nz* function is used to return a zero value if the combo box is empty. This isn't strictly needed (as the combo box in this application can never be empty) but it makes the sub more robust.

```
rs.FindFirst "[FilmID] = " & Str(Nz(Me![Combo21], 0))
```

For example:

If *Casablanca* had been chosen in the Combo Box the WHERE clause would be:

[FilmID] = 2

8 **Understand the recordset's EOF and Bookmark properties.**

EOF stands for End Of File. EOF will be set to True if the WHERE clause provided did not match any of the records in the recordset.

```
If Not rs.EOF Then Me.Bookmark = rs.Bookmark
```

This code is the same as (and could be re-written as):

```
If Not rs.EOF = True Then Me.Bookmark = rs.Bookmark
```

If EOF is not True we re-set the Form object's Bookmark property to match the cloned recordset's Bookmark property.

This causes the form to display the record that matches the value chosen within the combo box.

Lesson 6-6: Improve the combo box wizard code

note

When we created the combo box using the wizard the primary key (FilmID) was selected as the first field for the Combo Box Wizard – and then hidden later.

If this hadn't been done the *FindFirst* method would have compared the cloned recordset's *FilmTitleAndYear* field with the same calculated field in the form's recordset.

Our implementation is better because the *FindFirst* method is comparing the primary key from each recordset. This provides many advantages:

1/ The primary key field is always unique while the *FilmTitleAndYear* field could potentially contain duplicates.

2/ The comparison of two numbers is faster than comparing two long strings so the *FindFirst* method executes more quickly.

3/ If you use the non-preferred method (that will compare strings) there's a bug in the wizard code that will cause any string with apostrophes (such as *It's a Wonderful Life*) to crash Access when selected!

4/ The wizard will create the combo box with the *LimitToList* property set to *Yes* when the lookup is via a non-displayed primary key value. Using the non-preferred method this property will be set to *No* meaning that the user can type invalid values into the combo box.

5/ Primary and foreign keys are always indexed. Certain types of recordset also use indexes and it is possible that the recordset's *FindFirst* method (or a future version of the same) will be able to conduct an indexed search of the recordset leading to improved speed.

1   Open the frmFilm form in Design View.

2   Open the VBA Editor and inspect the code for the Find Film combo box's AfterUpdate event.

```
Private Sub Combo21_AfterUpdate()

' Find the record that matches the control.
Dim rs As Object

Set rs = Me.Recordset.Clone
rs.FindFirst "[FilmID] = " & Str(Nz(Me![Combo21], 0))

If Not rs.EOF Then Me.Bookmark = rs.Bookmark

End Sub
```

3   Remove dependence upon default properties.

The combo box wizard's code is heavily dependent upon default properties. This is poor programming practice as it isn't clear which properties are being manipulated (see sidebar). We have a clear rule defined for this (listed in *Appendix A: The Rules*) which states:

Never rely upon the default properties of objects.

Consider the code:

```
Str(Nz(Me![Combo21], 0))
```

The code is working with the *Value* property of the *Combo21* combo box control. It isn't clear that this is the case, however, as the code relies upon the reader knowing that the *Value* property is the default property of a combo box.

Re-write this line as:

```
Str(Nz(Me![Combo21].Value, 0))
```

4   Add error handling.

Strangely the wizard hasn't bothered to include any error handling code. This violates one of the programming standards defined for the project (listed in *Appendix A: The Rules*):

Error handling must be implemented in every sub without exception.

Add error handling by modifying the code as follows:

```
Private Sub Combo21_AfterUpdate()

On Error GoTo ErrorHandler

' Find the record that matches the control.
Dim rs As Object

Set rs = Me.Recordset.Clone
rs.FindFirst "[FilmID] = " & _
```

Important

Default properties

VBA has a very confusing "feature" in that every control has a default property.

cboCombo1.Value = "Test"

and

cboCombo1 = "Test"

...are functionally equivalent because *Value* is the default property of an Access *Combo Box* control.

The default property feature has (thankfully) been removed from the latest versions of stand-alone VB (VB.Net and VB 2005) showing that Microsoft also agree that it isn't the best feature in the world.

Never use default properties in your VBA code as they make the code less readable and more prone to error (as the actual property being manipulated must remain in the programmer's memory).

This information is provided so that you will understand code samples and code within existing applications as many non-professional programmers are extremely fond of using default properties.

This rule is included in *Appendix A: The Rules*.

```
Str(Nz(Me![Combo21].Value, 0))
If Not rs.EOF Then Me.Bookmark = rs.Bookmark

CleanUpAndExit:
Exit Sub

ErrorHandler:
    Call MsgBox("An error was encountered" & vbCrLf & _
    vbCrLf & _
    "Description: " & Err.Description & vbCrLf & _
    "Error Number: " & Err.Number, , "Error")

    Resume CleanUpAndExit
End Sub
```

Lesson 6-7: Correctly name controls

While the form wizard does many things really well it doesn't do a great job when it names bound controls such as the text boxes on the frmFilm form.

The Wizard simply gives the control exactly the same name as the underlying query field.

For example, the text box control bound to the FilmTitle field has been named FilmTitle. It is much better to have control names that make the type of control clear, such as *txtFilmTitle*.

Because of our *cradle to the grave naming convention* and consistent use of standard prefixes you'll find that there is only one possible logical name for each control.

In the case of the text box that is bound to the *FilmTitle* field the standard prefix of *txt* is added to the field name producing the name *txtFilmTitle*.

note

You could argue that the *Cradle to the Grave Naming Convention* demands that the foreign key combo boxes should be named cboMediaID etc.

The reason we've named them without the ID postfix is because the combo box actually contains a query including both the ID field and the field that will be displayed in the combo box from the related table.

The control is thus named using the name of the field that the combo box displays rather than the foreign key field name from the Film table.

1   Name the controls on the form as follows:

Control's Bound Field	Control Name
FilmTitle	txtFilmTitle
YearReleased	txtYearReleased
Rating	cboRating
FilmLengthMinutes	txtFilmLengthMinutes
MediaID	cboMedia
DirectorID	cboDirector
StudioID	cboStudio
FilmPlotOutline	txtFilmPlotOutline
FilmReview	txtFilmReview
FilmFrontCover	fraFilmFrontCover

The *Delete* button is already correctly named with the cmd prefix followed by the caption on the button itself (*cmdDelete*).

We haven't changed the name of the Find Film combo box. It would be nice to change it to *cboFindFilm* but because you'd also have to change code that referenced the present name it is easier to leave it with its generic name.

2   Generally accepted naming conventions.

While there is no strict standard for control naming conventions, generally accepted practice is to use the prefixes listed in the following table. These are also the prefixes used by Microsoft Consulting and published upon their web site.

These prefixes (and others) are re-stated in Appendix A – The Rules.

Prefix	Object Type	Example
cbo	Combo Box and Drop Down List Box	cboEnglish
chk	Checkbox	chkReadOnly
cmd	Command Button	cmdOK
ctr	Control (when specific type is unknown)	ctrCurrent
frm	Form	frmEntry
fra	Frame	fraStyle
img	Image	imgIcon
lbl	Label	lblHelpMessage
lin	Line	linVertical
lst	List Box	lstPolicyCodes
mnu	Menu	mnuFileOpen
opt	Option Button	optRed
pic	Picture	picHotel
txt	Text Box	txtLastName

Lesson 6-8: Program an add record button

Now that we have more of an insight into how the Command Button Wizard code works we'll add another button. This one is a little simpler than the Delete button. It will mimic the functionality of the existing *Add Record* button ▶✳ on the form's navigation bar. Once the *Add Record* button is added we can examine the code generated by the wizard.

1   With frmFilm in Design View add another command button to the form.

     The Command Button Wizard appears.

2   Choose the *Record Operations* category and the *Add New Record* action and then click the *Next* button.

3   Choose the *Text* option button and enter the text *&Add Record* to make the *A* key a hotkey and then click the *Next* button.

4   Name the button cmdAddRecord and click the Finish button.

5   Select the *Add Record* and *Delete Record* command buttons and then use the Format→Size and Format→Align commands on the main menu to make the buttons the same size and perfectly aligned.

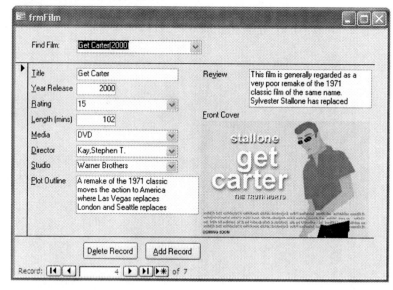

6   Test the new button.

     While the new button seems to work fine it has an annoying quirk in that the *cmdAddRecord* command button always has focus when it is clicked. This means that the user needs to click once more into the Title text box before adding a new film title.

     We can fix this by adding a little code.

7   View the code for the Add Record button's Click event handler.

Session6c

```
Private Sub cmdAddRecord_Click()
On Error GoTo Err_cmdAddRecord_Click

    DoCmd.GoToRecord , , acNewRec

Exit_cmdAddRecord_Click:

    Exit Sub

Err_cmdAddRecord_Click:

    MsgBox Err.Description
    Resume Exit_cmdAddRecord_Click

End Sub
```

8   Improve the error handling and set focus to the txtFilmTitle
     text box.

Modify the code as follows:

```
Private Sub cmdAddRecord_Click()

On Error GoTo Err_cmdAddRecord_Click

    DoCmd.GoToRecord , , acNewRec
    Me.txtFilmTitle.SetFocus

Exit_cmdAddRecord_Click:

    Exit Sub

Err_cmdAddRecord_Click:

Call MsgBox("An error was encountered" & vbCrLf & _

    vbCrLf & _
    "Description: " & Err.Description & vbCrLf & _
    "Error Number: " & Err.Number, , _
    "Error Adding Record")
    Resume Exit_cmdAddRecord_Click

End Sub
```

The txtFilmTitle text box's SetFocus method is used to place the
cursor into the form's first field to begin adding a new record.

9   Test the form.

Lesson 6-9: Handle the Form object's Current event

The Combo Box now provides a fast and robust method to quickly find any film in our database. While the combo box works just fine it looks a little unprofessional because it often contains text relating to a different film than the one currently on display in the form.

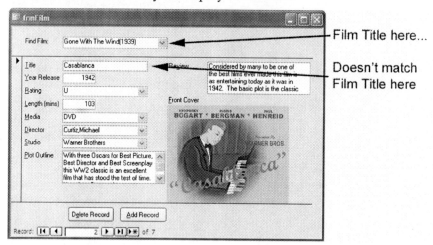

Film Title here...

Doesn't match Film Title here

This occurs when the user has moved to a different record using the bottom navigation buttons.

In this exercise we'll synchronise the Combo Box so that its contents are always in accord with the contents of the Title text box.

1   Open the Visual Basic code editor and create an event procedure for the Form object's Current event.

With the Visual Basic editor open select the Form object from the left hand drop-down list and the Current event from the right hand drop-down list. An event handler is created in the code window.

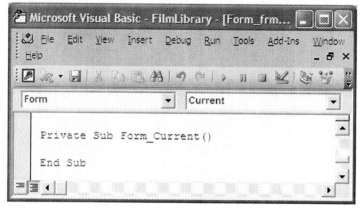

2   Edit the code to match the following.

```
Private Sub Form_Current()

Me.Combo21.Value = Me.FilmID

End Sub
```

Session6d

If you type *Me.Combo* you will see the one combo box we didn't correctly name. In this example the combo is called Combo21 but it is possible yours may have another name (such as Combo47).

The *Value* property of the Combo box object is its primary key and the command to the right of the assignment (=) operator (Me.FilmID) assigns the FilmID field from the Recordset object's currently displayed record to the combo box.

When the Combo Box object's primary key changes it will automatically update its Text property thus keeping the text shown in the Combo Box in harmony with the currently displayed record.

3   Test the Combo Box.

Return to Form View and try iterating through records using the navigation buttons. Notice how the value shown in the Combo Box changes as you navigate through the different Film records.

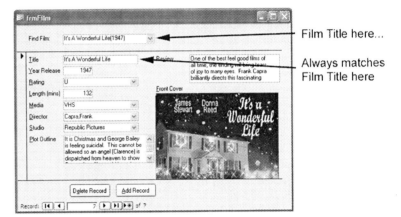

Film Title here...

Always matches Film Title here

Lesson 6-10: The Access object model revisited

Our examination of wizard generated code has led to the discovery of two new very important Access objects: the DoCmd and Recordset objects.

Let's now see how these objects fit into the Access Object Model.

note

ADO (ActiveX Data Objects)

It is possible (in Access 2002/2003 databases) to use ADO instead of DAO to access data stored in a regular Access (Jet) database but Microsoft do not recommend this approach.

Because the application developed within this book uses the Jet database we have used DAO rather than ADO to address the data within our code.

Since this is a "hot topic" amongst Access developers and widely debated we have reproduced Microsoft's advice below:

"Even though it is possible to bind a form to an ADO recordset that is using data from a Jet database, Microsoft recommends that you use DAO instead. DAO is highly optimized for Jet and typically performs faster than ADO when used with a Jet database".

Source: Article ID : 281998, Last Review : June 7, 2004, Revision 4.1

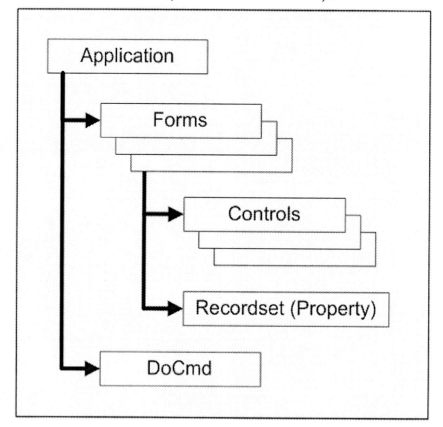

DAO (Data Access Objects)

Note that the Recordset property isn't really a part of the Access object model. It is really part of the DAO (Data Access Objects) object model.

The Recordset property of a Form object does, however, return a reference to the Recordset object that underpins the form so is shown above, more correctly, as a property of the Form object.

Session 6: Exercise

1   Create a new blank database named *Exercise6*.

2   Create a new form named *frmTest*.

3   Add four command buttons to the form with the captions *Ma&ximize, Mi&nimize, &Restore* and *&Close*, dismissing the command button wizard if it appears.

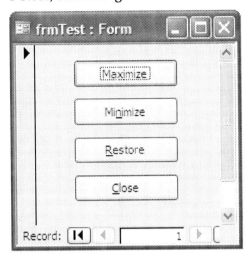

4   Name the four command buttons correctly.

When you have done this slide the page slightly to the left and view the Q4 answer to confirm that they are named correctly.

5   **Program the *Click* event for each button by implementing the required functionality using a method of the *DoCmd* object.**

The correct code can be viewed by sliding the page to the left and viewing the Q5 answer.

6   Test your form.

Exercise6

Q 5	Q 4
Each method of the DoCmd object can be called in a single line of code: ``` Private Sub cmdClose_Click() Call DoCmd.Close End Sub Private Sub cmdMaximize_Click() Call DoCmd.Maximize End Sub Private Sub cmdMinimize_Click() Call DoCmd.Minimize End Sub Private Sub cmdRestore_Click() Call DoCmd.Restore End Sub ```	The correct names for the controls can only be: cmdMaximize cmdMinimize cmdRestore cmdClose

Session Seven: Speeding up Data Entry

The secret isn't to work a lot, it's to work intelligently.

Vernon J. Hurst

It is often said that time is money. You can save an enormous amount of time for your data entry personnel if you optimise your forms for speed and empower your users to work smarter.

Effective database applications must enable users to quickly and intuitively find the record or records they are interested in. When dealing with small sets of test data you must always remember that the final application can potentially contain millions of records.

We get a fantastically useful and powerful filter feature for free when developing with Access. This is the built-in *Filter By Form* facility. In this session you'll learn how to make the form more *Filter By Form* friendly.

You'll also add an option group driven filter to allow the user to quickly filter by media type (DVD, VHS or All Media) with a single click.

Another way to speed things along is to provide interactive help so that the user is constantly aware of the type of information that should be entered into each field. You'll implement this with a context-sensitive help box to provide help information about the field that currently has focus.

You'll also provide the user with shortcut keys to automatically enter commonly required data, or sets of data, into the form with a single keystroke.

Session Objectives

By the end of this session you will be able to:

- Understand filtering events

- Add an option group control

- Set and remove filters using VBA code

- Understand how to program the *Enter* and *Exit* events attached to form controls

- Understand how to use the *Keydown* event to respond to keyboard input

Session7

Lesson 7-1: Filter using Filter by Form

Filter by form is a powerful Access feature that allows filtering by one or more fields on your form.

1 Open the frmFilm form in Form View.

2 Click the Filter by Form button 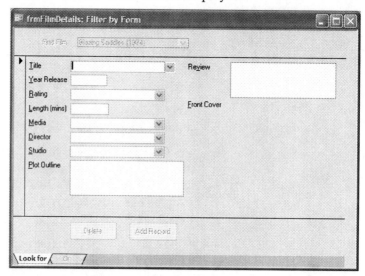 on the Form View toolbar.

A blank version of the form is displayed.

3 Click in the txtRating control and set a filter to only show U rated films.

Note that a drop down list is provided showing all unique values of the Rating field in the database.

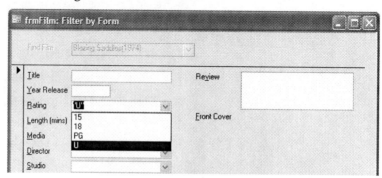

4 Click the Apply Filter button on the Form View toolbar.

The form now only displays films with a U rating. Note that it is clear that a filter is in action because the text at the bottom of the form includes the word *Filtered* and because the Apply Filter button now has a different appearance .

Session7

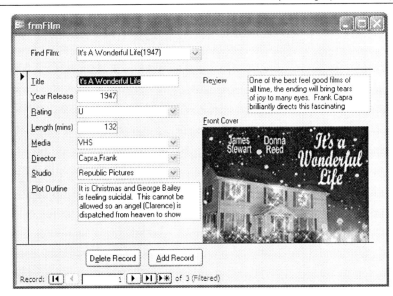

Filter by Form has worked perfectly but has introduced a new bug.

The Find Film combo box still displays all films but if a film that is not rated *U* is chosen it will not display in the form.

5 Disable the combo box if a filter is in effect.

The form has two important properties:

The *Filter* property determines the filter that will be applied (at the moment it contains the filter: *Rating = "U"*).

The *FilterOn* property determines whether the filter is active. It may have the values True or False.

In order to disable the Combo Box when a Filter is active we will once again use the form's *Current* event. This event occurs whenever the focus moves to a new record (making it the current record) or when the form is refreshed or re-queried.

Modify the code in the Form object's *Current* event handler as follows:

```
Private Sub Form_Current()

Me.Combo21.Value = Me.FilmID

If Me.FilterOn Then
    Me.Combo21.Enabled = False
Else
    Me.Combo21.Enabled = True
End If

End Sub
```

Note that your own *Find Film* combo box may have a slightly different name (such as *Combo27*).

6 Test the Form

When a filter is active the Combo Box is disabled and the contents are grayed out.

Lesson 7-2: Add an option group control

Because all of the films in the collection (at the moment) are VHS or DVD our users will appreciate a filter that with just one click is able to display a subset of films based upon the media. We will do this with an *Option Group* control.

1   Open up a little space at the bottom of the form by dragging the top border of the Form Footer bar downwards a little.

2   Click the Option Group control ![xyz] in the the control toolbox and then click and drag to draw an option group control beneath the *txtPlotOutline* text box.

The first screen of the Option Group Wizard is displayed.

3   Add three labels for the option buttons as shown and then click the Next button.

note

We are no longer able to take the first letter of each label name as a hotkey because they are already "taken" by another control on the form.

On very complex forms with many controls it is sometimes possible to "run out" of suitable hot keys for all controls.

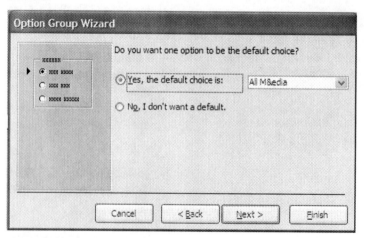

4   Keep *All Media* as the default choice and click the Next button.

5   Note the values assigned to each option and click the Next button.

Session7a

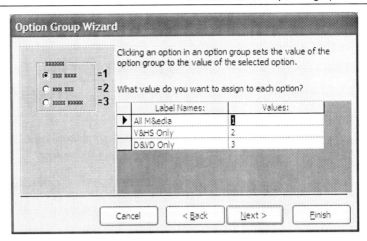

6   Retain the default option of *Save the value for later use* as, unlike the other controls, this control will not be bound to any field in the table. Press the *Next* button.

7   Stay with the defaults of *Option Buttons* and *Etched* then click the Next button.

8   Give the Option Group a caption of *Med&ia Type* and click the Finish button.

9   Bring up the Properties dialog for the new *Option Group* control (the option group control is a special type of frame control containing the option buttons) and set the *Name* property to *fraMediaType*

10 Test your new Option Group.

    Of course the Option Group doesn't actually do anything yet. We'll add functionality to the Option Group in the next lesson.

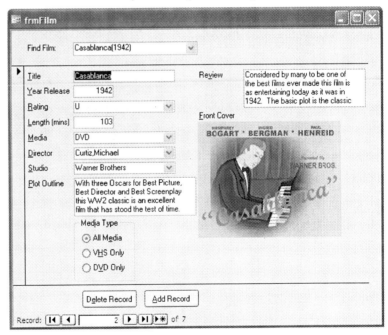

Lesson 7-3: Implement the option group control's functionality

1   Create an event handler for the Option Group control's *AfterUpdate* event.

Every time a user changes the currently selected option button within the Option Group the *AfterUpdate* event is triggered. This will be a perfect event for setting the form's filter to an appropriate value whenever the user clicks on an option button.

2   Add the following code to the Option Group control's AfterUpdate event.

```
Private Sub fraMediaType_AfterUpdate()

If Me.fraMediaType.Value = 2 Then

    Me.Filter = "Media = 'VHS'"
    Me.FilterOn = True

ElseIf Me.fraMediaType.Value = 3 Then

    Me.Filter = "Media = 'DVD'"
    Me.FilterOn = True

Else

    Me.FilterOn = False

End If

End Sub
```

The condition tests which option button is currently selected by examining the Option Group control's *Value* property.

The Value will be set to 2 if the VHS option is selected and to 3 if the DVD option is selected.

Any other value will show *All Media* by switching the filter off.

3   Test the Form.

Testing the form reveals a small problem.

When the user has a *Filter by Form* filter active and then applies a *Media Type* filter using the option group the result may not be what is expected. This is because the second filter over-writes and replaces the first.

The user will intuitively know how the filter works if we simply disable the option group filter facility whenever a *Filter by Form* filter is active.

4   Add the following code to the form's *ApplyFilter* event handler:

```
Private Sub Form_ApplyFilter(Cancel As Integer,
ApplyType As Integer)
```

Session7b

```
If ApplyType = acShowAllRecords Then
    Me.fraMediaType.Value = 1 ' Show all films

    Me.fraMediaType.Enabled = True
Else
    Me.fraMediaType.Value = Null ' No option button
                                ' selected
    Me.fraMediaType.Enabled = False
End If
End Sub
```

The Form's *ApplyFilter* event is triggered whenever a filter is applied to the form using an Access feature such as *Filter By Form* but not when a filter is applied by VBA code.

When the event occurs the option group (fraMediaType) has its default property set to Null (see sidebar) and is disabled.

5   Test the form.

Open the form in Form View and use Filter By Form to filter down to only show films that are 18 rated. Note that the option group is now grayed out and that no option is selected.

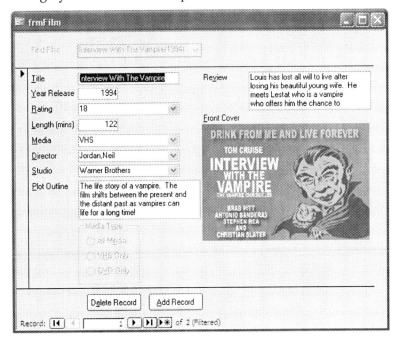

Lesson 7-4: Add interactive help

Every control has an *Enter* and *Exit* event. These events are very useful as they allow you to know programmatically which control the user is currently editing.

We're going to use these events to provide a window that will display interactive help for the control that has focus.

1   Add a label control to the form.

Place the control in the position shown below and type the word *test* into the control for now (Access refuses to create label controls with blank captions).

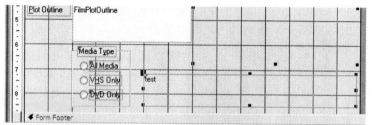

2   Set the label's *Border Style* property to *Solid*.

The label border is now visible.

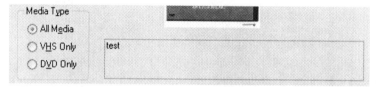

3   Remove the word test from the *Caption* property and set the *Name* property to *lblHelp*.

The word *test* was only put into the Caption property because Access will not create a label control with a blank caption. Once created, however, Access is happy for you to set the Caption property back to blank.

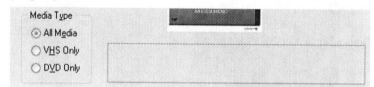

4   Add the following code to the cboRating control's Enter event handler.

```
Private Sub cboRating_Enter()

Me.lblHelp.Caption = "BBFC types should be used " & _
"wherever possible.  At present these are:" & _
"Uc, U, PG, 12A, 12, 15, 18 and R18."

End Sub
```

5   Add the following code to the cboRating control's Exit event.

```
Private Sub cboRating_Exit(Cancel As Integer)
```

Session7c

```
Me.lblHelp.Caption = ""

End Sub
```

6   Test the help feature for the cboRating control.

Switch into Form View and click or tab into the cboRating combo box. While the cboRating control has focus you can view the help for the control.

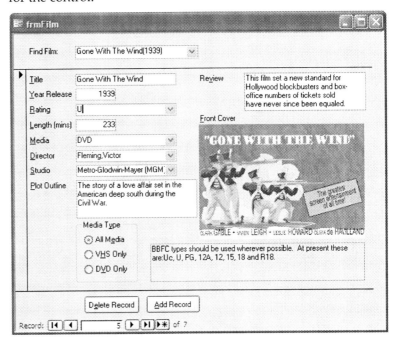

Lesson 7-5: Add a shortcut hotkey to a control

note

Bit masks

You may wonder why the constant for the control key is named: *acCtrlMask* instead of *vbControKey*.

The answer is that this is a special type of constant called a bit mask.

Without dwelling upon the science behind bit masks it is sufficient to say that they are constants that can be added together to test for multiple conditions. The three bit masks that are of interest for the KeyDown event are:

acShiftMask - the SHIFT key.
acCtrlMask – the CTRL key.
acAltMask - the ALT key.

If you wanted to test for the user holding the <Shift>+<Ctrl> keys down together you'd use code such as this:-

```
IF Shift = _
acShiftMask + _
acCtrlMask Then
...
```

1   Add the following code to the *txtFilmYearReleased* control's *KeyDown* event handler.

```
Private Sub txtFilmYearReleased_KeyDown(KeyCode As
Integer, Shift As Integer)

' Ctrl-1 to Ctrl-9 = years 2001 to 2009

If KeyCode >= vbKey1 And KeyCode <= vbKey9 And _
Shift = acCtrlMask Then

    Me.txtFilmYearReleased.Value = "200" & _
CStr(KeyCode - vbKey0)

End If

End Sub
```

The *KeyDown* event occurs when the user presses a key on the keyboard. It has two arguments.

The *KeyCode* argument passes the code number of the keyboard key that the user has pressed. The constant vbKey1 corresponds to the number <1> on the keyboard.

The *Shift* argument indicates whether the user is holding down the <Shift>, <Ctrl>,<Alt> or any combination of these keys. (When the *Shift* argument is equal to the constant *acCtrlMask* we know that the <Ctrl> key was held down).

The expression KeyCode - vbKey0 works because the keycodes for keys 0 to 9 ascend numerically in increments of one.

2   Add some interactive help to inform the user of the choices available.

Add the following code to the txtFilmYearReleased text box's Enter and Exit events.

```
Private Sub txtFilmYearReleased_Enter()

Me.lblHelp.Caption= "Enter year in full eg: 1997. " & _
"For years 2001-2009 you may use the " & _
"shortcut keys Ctr-1 through Ctrl-9."

End Sub

Private Sub txtFilmYearReleased_Exit(Cancel As Integer)

Me.lblHelp.Caption = ""

End Sub
```

3   Test the form.

Switch into Form View and click the Add Record button. Click or tab into the txtFilmYearReleased text box. While the txtFilmYearReleased control has focus context-sensitive help is displayed.

Session7d

Try pressing the <Ctrl> key plus any of the number keys <1> to <9> on the keyboard. Note that the shortcut works exactly as described.

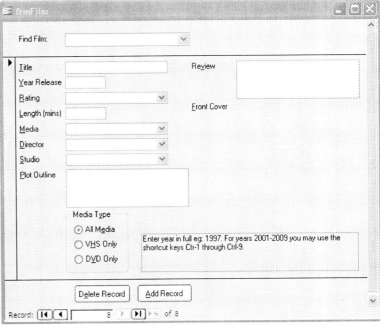

Session 7: Exercise

1   Create a new blank database named *Exercise7*.

2   Create a new form named *frmTest*.

3   Add three text box controls to the form with the captions First Name, Last Name and Telephone Number.

4   Name the three text boxes correctly.

      Slide the page slightly to the left and view the Q4 answer to confirm that they are named correctly.

5   It is possible to change the background color of a *Textbox* control by changing its *BackColor* property. There are several standard vb constants to easily set common colors such as *vbYellow* and *vbWhite*.

      Program each Textbox's *Enter* and *Exit* event handler so that the *BackColor* property is changed to *vbYellow* when the control has focus and *vbWhite* when the control loses focus. The correct code can be viewed by sliding the page to the left and viewing the Q5 answer.

6   Test your form.

      As you move between the Textboxes the currently active Textbox is always yellow while the other two text boxes are white.

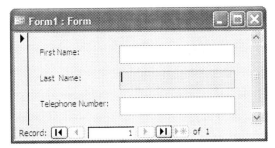

7   When a Textbox's *KeyDown* event is triggered a *KeyCode* argument is passed to the event handler for the key being pressed and a *Shift* argument to indicate whether the *Shift*, *Control* or *Alt* key is being held down.

      For the <Alt>+<n> combination the following arguments are passed to the *KeyDown* event handler:

      Keycode = vbKeyN   Shift = acAltMask

      Use this information to program the *txtTelephoneNumber* Textbox's *KeyDown* event handler so that the text "Not Known" is automatically entered when the user presses <Alt>+<n> and the *txtTelephoneNumber* text box has focus. View the Q6 answer if you have difficulty implementing this.

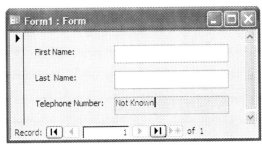

Exercise7

Session 7: Exercise answers

Q 6	Q 5	Q 4
| ```
Private Sub txtTelephoneNumber_KeyDown(KeyCode As Integer, Shift As Integer)
If KeyCode = vbKeyN And Shift = acAltMask Then
    Me.txtTelephoneNumber.Value = "Not Known"

End If
``` | Each Textbox needs to have the color set as in the example code below for the txtFirstName text box.<br><br>```
Private Sub txtFirstName_Enter()
Me.txtFirstName.BackColor = vbYellow
End Sub

Private Sub txtFirstName_Exit(Cancel As Integer)
Me.txtFirstName.BackColor = vbWhite
End Sub
``` | The correct names for the controls can only be:<br><br>txtFirstName<br><br>txtLastName<br><br>txtTelephoneNumber |

Session Eight: Implementing A Popup Browse Form

> Progress isn't made by early risers. It's made by lazy men trying to find easier ways to do something.
>
> *Robert Heinlein, Time Enough for Love,*
> *US science fiction author (1907 – 1988)*

Most database applications consist of a data store (containing the tables and data), and a collection of forms to maintain the data.

Programmers call these forms *Add/Edit/Delete* or *CRUD* (Create, Read, Update, and Delete) forms.

The form needs to efficiently Add, Edit and Delete records and must allow the user to quickly locate the record that needs to be Edited or Deleted.

The generic Access approach is to use a navigation bar (only useful for very small data sets) and the *Filter By Form* facility (useful for data sets of any size) to locate a specific record.

This can work well but many commercial applications (whether or not they are written in Access) take a two-form approach.

The two-form approach splits the *Finding* of the record and the *Edit and Delete* functions.

We're not going to convert the main form of this application to the two-form paradigm. We will instead implement an *Advanced Find* form that will allow the user to select a record from a scrolling browse list of all records in the Film table.

If you like this approach you shouldn't have any difficulty in creating an application that uses the two-form paradigm as you'll already understand all of the required techniques.

Session Objectives

By the end of this session you will be able to:

■ Use a listbox control to browse a dataset

■ Convert a form to a dialog box

■ Use the Recordset object's FindFirst method

■ Understand and use the Recordset object's Bookmark property

■ Understand and use the Recordset object's Clone method

■ Understand modal and modeless forms

■ Pass information between forms

Session8

Lesson 8-1: Create a browse form using a listbox control

1   Click the *Queries* object in the Database window and then copy your general-purpose *qryFilmDetails* query and paste it with the new name *qryFilmDetailsForListBox*.

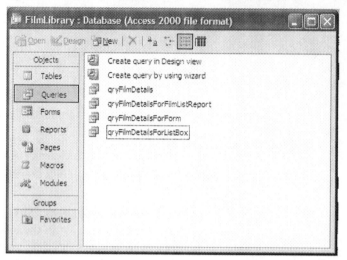

2   Click the *Forms* object in the Database window and then double-click *Create form in Design view.*

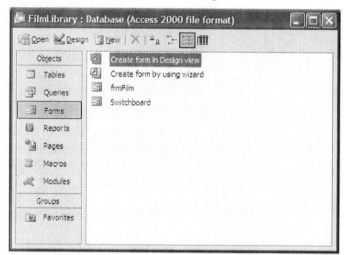

3   Save the new form with the name frmFindFilm.

4   Make your form a little wider and deeper and add a list box control to it.

The first screen of the List Box Wizard is displayed.

5   Choose *I want the list box to look up values in a table or query* and click the Next button.

6   Click the Queries option button and choose the query you have just created: qryFilmDetailsForListBox.

7   Click the Next button and select the following fields in the order listed:

Session8

important

Because of the way Microsoft have implemented the ListBox control's recordset it is necessary to include the primary key within the selected fields even though this is already included in qryFilmDetailsForListBox.

As the primary key should always be meaningless there's no point in showing it to the user so we keep it hidden by reducing the *FilmId* primary key's column width to zero.

8   Click the Next button. You don't need to define a sort order as the query already sorts by Film Title and Year Released.

9   Click the Next button and set appropriate column widths. Make the FilmID column zero width as its contents are meaningless (see sidebar). You don't need to make the columns wide enough to accommodate the field names as the List Box control doesn't support column headers. (If they were required you'd have to implement them using label controls).

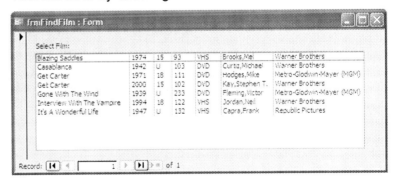

10   Click the Next button and Choose FilmID as the value that you want to store. This will be used later to find the matching record to display in frmFilm.

11   Label the List Box's Caption property *Select Film:* and then click the Finish button.

12   Move the label (with the caption *Select Film*) so that it is above the top left corner of the list box.

13   Set the List Box control's Name property to lstFilm.

14   Test the form by showing it in Form View.

The form is working well but the navigation bar and some other details are redundant. In the next lesson we'll remove some of these items and convert the form into a dialog box.

Lesson 8-2: Convert a form to a dialog box

Dialog boxes are everywhere in Windows. The MsgBox function produces a dialog box:

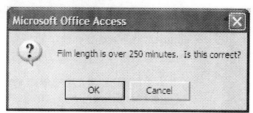

An example of a more complicated dialog box is the dialog you see when you try to print.

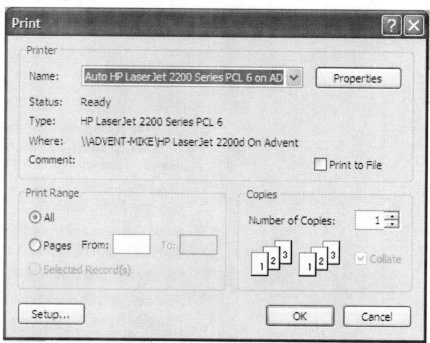

At the moment our form looks nothing like the dialog boxes users are accustomed to.

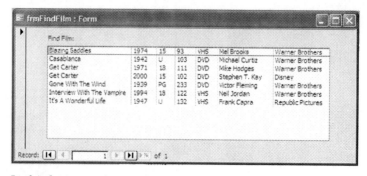

In this lesson we're going to convert it so that it will look just like any other Windows dialog box. All that is needed is to set a few form properties.

Session8a

1   Bring up the frmFindFilm form properties dialog and set the following properties:

Property	Value
Caption	Find Film
Scroll Bars	Neither
Record Selectors	No
Navigation Buttons	No
Dividing Lines	No
Auto Center	Yes
Border Style	Dialog
Min Max Buttons	None
PopUp	Yes
Modal	Yes

tip

Adjusting the display size of a dialog box form

If you have set the Border Style of a form to Dialog and you find you need to re-size it you'll have to do this in Design View.

Most of these properties are self-explanatory but the *PopUp* and *Modal* properties require further explanation.

The PopUp property ensures that the popped-up form is *always on top* (it cannot be hidden or obscured by any other form including the form that invoked it).

The Modal property is also usually set for PopUp forms. A modal form prevents any other interaction with the application until it is closed.

In contrast, *Modeless* forms (the Access default setting) allow the user to freely switch focus between them so that many forms can be worked with at the same time without closing any of them.

2 Switch to Form View and notice the changes to the form.

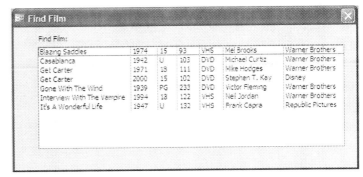

The form now looks exactly the same as any other Windows dialog box.

Lesson 8-3: Use the recordset object's FindFirst and Clone methods and Bookmark property.

1   Add a command button to the form but dismiss the Wizard by clicking the Cancel button when it appears.

2   Set the Properties of the new button as follows:

Property	Value
Name	cmdShowSelectedFilm
Caption	&Show Selected Film
Default	Yes
Enabled	No

3   Add another command button but this time let the Wizard create it for you. Choose the following wizard options:

Wizard option	Setting
Category	Form Operations
Actions	Close form
Caption	Text caption of &Cancel
Name	cmdCancel

4   Set the Cancel propety of the new button to Yes. This will enable the <Escape key> to cancel the form (see sidebar).

5   Use the main menu Format→Align and Format→Size options to make the buttons of identical size and perfectly aligned so that your form looks like the following:

6   Add the following code to the cmdShowSelectedFilm command button's Click event:

```
Private Sub cmdShowSelectedFilm_Click()

Dim rs As DAO.Recordset
Set rs = Forms!frmFilm.RecordsetClone

Call rs.FindFirst("FilmID =" & Me.lstFilm.Value)
Forms!frmFilm.Recordset.Bookmark = rs.Bookmark
Call DoCmd.Close(acForm, "frmFindFilm")

End Sub
```

Session8b

How the code works:

```
Dim rs As DAO.Recordset
Set rs = Forms!frmFilm.RecordsetClone
```

A recordset object is created that is a clone of the recordset object underpinning the frmFilm form (the form must be open for this to work but as this form will always be opened from a command button on frmFilm, this will always be the case).

```
Call rs.FindFirst("FilmID =" & Me.lstFilm.Value)
```

The FindFirst method of the cloned recordset object is used to find the record that matches the FilmID field of the currently selected record within the ListBox control.

```
Forms!frmFilm.Recordset.Bookmark = rsBookmark
```

The frmFilm form's Bookmark property is set to match the Bookmark property of the cloned recordset object. This will cause frmFilm's current record to match the record chosen in the listbox control.

```
Call DoCmd.Close(acForm, "frmFindFilm")
```

The pop-up form frmFindFilm is closed leaving frmFilm on the screen with the chosen record displayed.

7 **Enable the cmdShowSelectedFilm command button when the user has selected a record.**

Add the following code to the List Box control's AfterUpdate event:

```
Private Sub lstFilm_AfterUpdate()

Me.cmdShowSelectedFilm.Enabled = True

End Sub
```

The reason that the cmdShowSelectedFilm command button's *Enabled* property was set to *No* was so that the user could not try to show a film record prior to actually selecting one. The AfterUpdate method will trigger as soon as the user selects a film within the list box.

8 **Enable double-clicking the list box as an alternative way to invoke cmdShowSelectedFilm.**

We can save the user time by adding the following code to the List Box control's DblClick event:

```
Private Sub lstFilm_DblClick(Cancel As Integer)

If Not IsNull(Me.lstFilm.Value) Then
    Call cmdShowSelectedFilm_Click
End If

End Sub
```

Testing that the lstFilm control's *Value* property (the FilmID) is not *Null* is really not required since a primary key can never be Null but adds robustness to the code. Anticipating the impossible is always a good idea when programming!

Lesson 8-4: Launch the popup form from the main form

The frmFindFilm form has been designed to add functionality to the frmFilm form rather than to function as a stand-alone form.

If the frmFilm form was not open and an attempt was made to use the frmFindFilm form stand-alone, a run-time error would result as it would be impossible to clone a recordset object from a form that did not exist.

In this lesson you will add a command button to the frmFilm form that will open the frmFindFilm form when clicked.

1   Open the frmFilm form in Design Mode and add a command button just to the right of the cboFindFilm combo box.

The first screen of the Command Button Wizard appears.

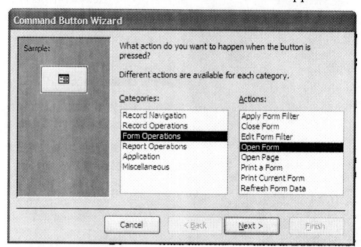

2   Choose the Category:*Form Operations* and the Action:*Open Form* and click the Next button.

3   Choose frmFindFilm as the form you want the button to open and click the Next button.

4   Give the form a text caption of Adva&nced Find and click the Next button.

5   Name the button cmdAdvancedFind and click the Finish Button.

The form should now look like this:

Session8c

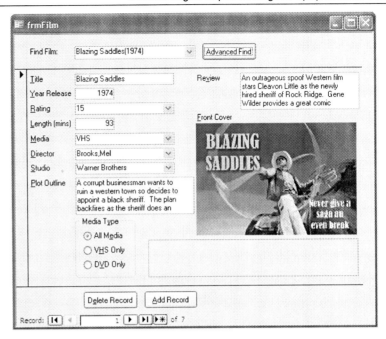

6 Test your form

Click the Advanced Find button. The FindFilm browse dialog pops up.

Note that this is a modal dialog so you cannot do anything with frmFilm until it is closed.

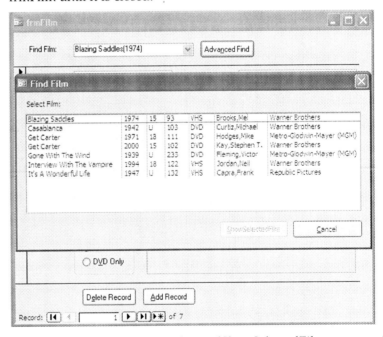

Click on any film in the list. The cmdShowSelectedFilm command button becomes enabled.

Test both clicking the *Show Selected Film* button and double-clicking a film. You are returned to the main frmFilm form with the selected film displayed.

Test using the <Enter> and <Escape> keys on the frmFindFilm form. They have exactly the same effect as clicking the *Show Selected Film* and *Cancel* buttons.

Session 8: Exercise

1 Create a new blank database named *Exercise8*.

2 Create two new forms named *frmTest* and *frmPopUp*. Set each form's *Navigation Buttons* property to *No*.

3 Add a command button to *frmTest* and use the command button Wizard to make it open the *frmPopUp* form. Give the button a caption of *&Pop Up Form* and a name of *cmdPopUpForm*.

4 Add a text box control to *frmTest*. Give it's label the caption property *From Pop Up:* and name the text box txtFromPopup. Set the *Locked* property of the text box to *Yes*.

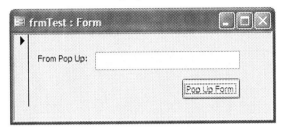

5 Add a command button to the *frmPopUp* form and use the command button wizard to make it close the form. Set the command button's Caption property to *Send Back Text* and the Name property to *cmdSendBackText*.

6 Add a text box to the *frmPopUp* form. Give it's label the caption *Text To Send Back:* and name it *txtTextToSendBack*.

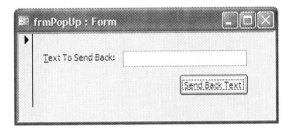

7 Add some code to the *cmdSendBackText* command button's *Click* event that will take any text that is in the *txtTextToSendBack* text box and send it to the *txtFromPopUp* text box in *frmTest* before closing the form.

If you are unable to write some code that works turn the page to view a code listing.

8 Test the forms.

Open *frmTest* and click the *PopUpForm* command button. When the *frmPopUpForm* appears enter some text into the *txtTextToSendBack* text box. When you click the cmdSendBackText command button the text should appear in the *txtFromPopUp* text box on *frmTest*.

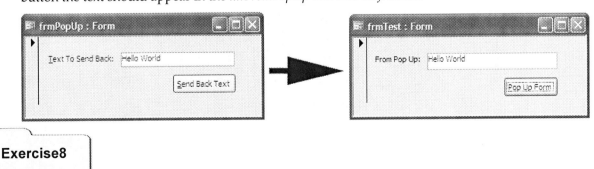

Exercise8

Session 8: Exercise answers

```
Private Sub cmdSendBackText_Click()
On Error GoTo Err_cmdSendBackText_Click

    Forms!frmTest.txtFromPopUp.Value = Me.txtTextToSendBack.Value

    DoCmd.Close

Exit_cmdSendBackText_Click:
    Exit Sub

Err_cmdSendBackText_Click:
    MsgBox Err.Description
    Resume Exit_cmdSendBackText_Click

End Sub
```

Session Nine: Maintaining Static Data

They always say time changes things, but you actually have to change them yourself.

Andy Warhol, The Philosophy of Andy Warhol,
US artist (1928 - 1987)

One of the features that is most-requested by users is a simple way of updating Static Data. The term Static Data is used to refer to data that is not normally expected to change on a regular basis but, as Andy Warhol points out, a method is needed to allow users to change static data when requirements change.

In our application a good example of Static Data would be the different film ratings. The British Board of Film Classification grades UK films into the following ratings:

Perhaps they will add other classifications in the future. This would result in the user having to edit the static data in the Rating table.

One approach would be to provide the user with a simple update form for the Rating, Media and Studio tables but, thanks to VBA, we can provide a much more efficient method by creating self-updating combo boxes that allow all static data to be maintained from the main frmFilm form.

In the case of the cboDirector combo we can't take this approach because the Director's name isn't a simple field but a concatenation of DirectorFirstName and DirectorLastName. In this case we'll provide a pop-up form to allow the user to add new directors.

Session Objectives

By the end of this session you will be able to:

■ Create self-updating bound combo boxes

■ Create and use a global constant

■ Create and use a globally visible utility function

■ Create a pop-up form to add static data with multiple fields

■ Use the Requery method to refresh a control's recordset

■ Make SQL expressions "Apostrophe Safe"

Session9

Lesson 9-1: Create a self updating bound combo box

1   Open the frmFilm form and click the Add Record button.

2   Enter *Test Film* in the *Film Title* text box.

3   Imagine that this is your first Blu-ray film and you need a new Media type. Type *Blu-ray* into the Media combo box.

4   The following error message is displayed.

5   Add the following code to the cboMedia combo box control's NotInList event.

```
Private Sub cboMedia_NotInList(NewData As String,
Response As Integer)

Dim mbxResponse As VbMsgBoxResult
Dim strSQL As String

mbxResponse = MsgBox("Are you sure you want to add " &
NewData & _
" as a valid media type?", vbQuestion + vbYesNo)

If mbxResponse = vbYes Then

    strSQL = "INSERT INTO Media([Media]) " & _
    "VALUES('" & NewData & "');"
    Call DoCmd.SetWarnings(False)
    Call DoCmd.RunSQL(strSQL)
    Call DoCmd.SetWarnings(True)
    Call MsgBox( _
    "The new media type has been added to the database."
_   , vbInformation)
    Response = acDataErrAdded
Else
    Response = acDataErrDisplay
End If
End Sub
```

note

Bit masks

You may wonder why you are able to add the *vbQuestion* and *vbYesNo* constants together to provide a single argument that will result in a Yes/No message box showing a Question icon.

The answer is that these are special types of constants called bit masks.

Without dwelling upon the science behind bit masks it is sufficient to say that they are constants that can be added together to test for multiple conditions.

How the code works:

The combo box control's *NotInList* event triggers when the user enters a value into a combo box that is not valid, The *NewData* argument contains the text that was typed into the combo box and the *Response* argument is used as a return value to tell Access what to do when the Subroutine ends.

Session9

```
mbxResponse = MsgBox("Are you sure you want to add " & _
NewData & _
" as a valid media type?", vbQuestion + vbYesNo)
```

A message box is used to ask the user to confirm that the new media type should be added to the media table. The user's response is stored in the *mbxResponse* variable.

```
If mbxResponse = vbYes Then

    strSQL = "INSERT INTO Media([Media]) " & _
    "VALUES('" & NewData & "');"
```

If the user confirms that the data should be added a standard SQL action query is generated by the above code. For example:

INSERT INTO Media([Media]) VALUES ('Blu-ray');

```
Call DoCmd.SetWarnings(False)
```

The *SetWarnings* method of the DoCmd object is used to switch off standard Access warnings.

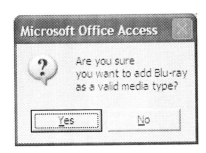

```
Call DoCmd.RunSQL(strSQL)
```

The SQL action query is then executed using the DoCmd object's *RunSQL* method.

```
Call DoCmd.SetWarnings(True)
```

Warnings are switched back on again using the DoCmd object's SetWarnings method.

```
    Call MsgBox("The new media type has been added " & _
"to the database." , vbInformation)
```

A message box is displayed advising the user that the new media type was added.

```
Response = acDataErrAdded
```

The *Response* return value is set to the VB constant *acDataErrAdded* to inform Access that data has been added to the table providing data to the combo box. This will cause Access to requery the combo box's recordset object when the new value will be available in the list.

```
Else
    Response = acDataErrDisplay
End If
```

If the user does not want to add the data the Response return value is set to the VB constant *acDataErrDisplay* meaning that Access should display its usual error message.

6   Test your self-updating combo box.

   Add a new media type by entering the value in the Media combo box. Confirm that the new media type was added by viewing the Media table in Datasheet view.

7   Use the same technique to make cboRating and cboStudio into self-updating combo boxes.

   Cut and paste the code from the *cboMedia_NotInList* event handler to the *cboRating_NotInList* and *cboStudio_NotInList* event handlers. You'll only need to change a few words in each block of code.

Lesson 9-2: Make the combo box accept apostrophes

Understanding the problem

A common problem with all SQL based code is the handling of apostrophes. Try to add a new media called 8mm 'Super 8'. The error handler produces the following message:

note

The reason that the message is so user-unfriendly is that we've yet to add error handling code to the NotInList event handlers.

This will be rectified when we QA (Quality Assure) the application in a later session.

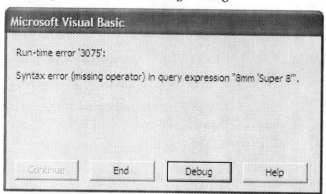

While a normal Access form will transparently handle apostrophes we need to manually correct them when creating SQL expressions within VBA Code.

The problem is caused by invalid SQL syntax. For example, consider the following code in the event handler

```
strSQL = "INSERT INTO Media([Media]) " & _
"VALUES ('" & NewData & "');"
```

If the Media field contains the value 8mm the code will produce the SQL query:

```
INSERT INTO MEDIA([Media]) VALUES ('8mm')
```

… And all works perfectly, but change it to 8mm 'Super 8 ' and the code produces the following SQL query :

```
INSERT INTO MEDIA([Media]) VALUES ('8mm 'Super 8'')
```

As you can see, the apostrophes are now confusing and don't make sense to the SQL interpreter causing the error.

A peculiarity of SQL syntax is that two apostrophes within a block of text ('') are always processed without error in the same way as one('). This means that a simple search and replace of one apostrophe for two would fix the problem.

The following SQL query is valid syntax and executes without error:

```
INSERT INTO MEDIA([Media]) VALUES ('8mm''Super 8''')
```

While the above code works it is difficult to read and prone to coding errors. A much better solution is to develop a library function (a general purpose function we can re-use over and over) to elegantly convert the SQL for us.

Session9a

1   Open the code editor and select Insert→Module from the main menu.

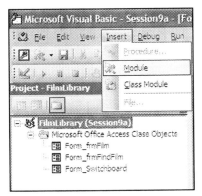

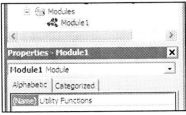

note

If you can't see the Explorer or Properties windows.

If either the *Project Explorer Window* or the *Properties Window* are not visible within the VBA editor select *View →Project Explorer* and/or *View →Properties Window* from the editor's main menu to bring them back.

A new module called *Module1* appears in the *Project Explorer* window attached to a new folder called *Modules*.

2   Rename Module1 to *Utility Functions*.

Click on Module1 in the explorer window and note the properties window below. Change the *Name* property to *Utility Functions*.

3   Code the utility function.

Add the following code to the Utility Functions module:

```
Function SQLSafe(strSQL As String)

If strSQL <> "" Then
    strSQL = Replace(strSQL, Chr(39), Chr(39) & Chr(39))
End If

SQLSafe = strSQL

End Function
```

It can be seen that this code uses the Visual Basic Replace() function to substitute one apostrophe (ASCII 39) with two.

4   Use the SQLSafe function to clean up the text passed to the *cboMedia_NotInList* event handler.

We now only need add a single line of code to the event handler to replace any single apostrophes in the passed media type with double apostrophes thus converting it to valid SQL syntax:

```
Private Sub cboMedia_NotInList(NewData As String,
Response As Integer)

Dim mbxResponse As VbMsgBoxResult
Dim strSQL As String

mbxResponse = MsgBox("Are you sure you want to add " &
NewData & _
" as a valid media type?", vbQuestion + vbYesNo)

If mbxResponse = vbYes Then

    NewData = SQLSafe(NewData)

    strSQL = "INSERT INTO Media([Media]) " & _
    "VALUES('" & NewData & "');"

    Call DoCmd.SetWarnings(False)
```

Remainder of code not shown.

5   Test your code.

You'll now find that apostrophes within media names cause no problems at all.

6   Make the *cboRating* and *cboStudio* combo boxes SQL safe by adding the same line of code to their NotInList event handlers.

Lesson 9-3: Create and use a global constant

note

Globally visible constants are used by most programmers but shouldn't be confused with globally visible variables.

Most professional programmers would *never* use globally visible variables as they violate the principle of encapsulation and can introduce a whole new class of difficult-to-fix bugs into your code.

note

It is a good idea to prefix any globally visible constants with a name that is very unlikely to clash with variables created by any other programmer.

Because the constant is visible everywhere there is a possibility that the name will clash with a Local or Module scoped variable name. We use two coding standards to make this (almost) impossible.

1/ Constants are the only variable type that may contain underscores. They are also spelt in ALL CAPITALS so that you are always aware that you are dealing with constants within your code. Note that Microsoft do not use this convention with their own constants such as *vbRed*.

2/ A prefix that is very unlikely to be used by any third party code is used for all constants. We are using *TSM_* as our prefix (Microsoft use *vb*).

A constant is a special type of variable that can never change its value. The word *Global* is used to describe the scope of the constant, meaning that it is visible everywhere within the application.

Global Constants such as *vbRed* are defined within the VBA programming language to make code more readable.

We'll create a global constant to store the name, version number and status of the application in a single location so that when future versions are released this information can be easily updated.

1   Open the Utility Functions module.

2   Add a constant to the module to store the application name and version.

Add the following code to the top of the module, just below Option Explicit.

```
Public Const TSM_APPLICATION_NAME As String  = _
"Film Library Manager Version 1.0 alpha"
```

3   Open the frmFilm code module.

Do this from within the editor by double-clicking the frmFilm object in the Project Explorer window. If the Project Explorer window isn't visible you can enable it by selecting *View →Project Explorer* from the main menu.

4   Add an event handler for the Form's Load event.

Do this by selecting *Form* from the left hand drop-down list and *Load* from the right hand drop-down list at the top of the code window.

5   Set the form's caption to display the contents of the global constant.

The Form_Load event triggers as the form loads but before it is displayed on the screen. It is a great place to set up such things as captions in code.

6   Add the following code to the Form's Load event:

```
Private Sub Form_Load()

Me.Caption = TSM_APPLICATION_NAME & " - Add/Edit/Delete Films"

End Sub
```

7   Test the form.

When the form is opened the application name stored in the global constant is displayed in the top left-hand corner followed by the form's purpose.

Session9b

note

alpha, beta and release candidate versions

When an application is under construction it is usually called an *alpha version*.

When an application is finished but untested, or partially tested, it is usually called a *beta version*.

It is common to make beta test versions available to interested users so that they can report problems.

As users report problems during testing the beta version has a build number incremented, for example: *beta build 27, beta build 28* etc.

Because fixing bugs can often introduce other bugs, (sometimes more serious than the bug that was fixed), very stable beta builds are shortlisted as *release candidates*. When the business is ready to go live one of the release candidates is selected as the final release version.

Managers often pressure programmers to release untested beta versions for actual use in the business. This is usually a very bad idea if the application is mission critical (vital to the success of the business).

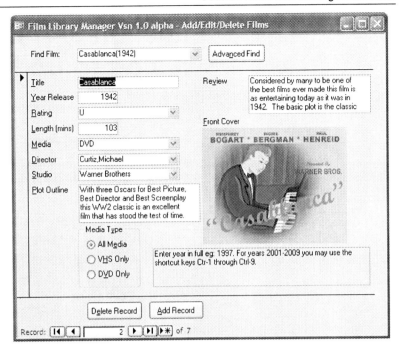

8   Modify the frmFindFilm form in the same way by adding the following code to its Form_Load event handler.

```
Private Sub Form_Load()

Me.Caption = TSM_APPLICATION_NAME & " - Advanced Find"

End Sub
```

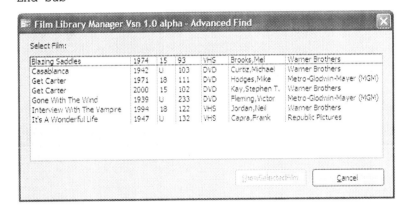

Lesson 9-4: Create a popup dialog to update related data

By converting the combo boxes to self-updating combo boxes we've given the user a fast and convenient way to add Media, Studio and Rating records directly from the frmFilm form.

Because the Director table has two fields (DirectorFirstName and DirectorLastName) we can't use a self-updating combo box to maintain Director information.

In this lesson we're going to add a popup dialog form that will allow the user to quickly and simply maintain director names from the frmFilm form.

The popup form won't need the functionality of a regular Add/Edit/Delete form since its only purpose is to allow the user to add a single Director record to the Director table.

1   Click the Forms object in the Database window and then double click *Create form by using wizard.*

2   Choose the Director table and the fields *DirectorFirstName* and *DirectorLastName* (we have no interest in displaying the DirectorID primary key as its value is meaningless to the user).

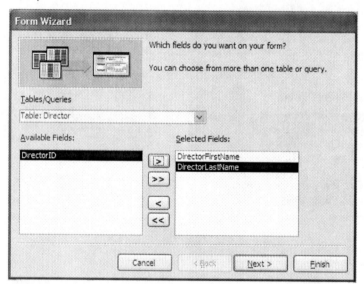

3   Click the Next button twice to accept the default *Columnar* Layout and *Standard* style and then name the form *frmAddDirector.*

4   Convert the form to a popup modal dialog by setting the following properties:

Session9c

Property	Value
Caption	Add Director
Scroll Bars	Neither
Record Selectors	No
Navigation Buttons	No
Dividing Lines	No
Auto Center	Yes
Border Style	Dialog
Min Max Buttons	None
PopUp	Yes
Modal	Yes

5   Name the two textbox controls correctly as txtDirectorFirstName and txtDirectorLastName.

6   Add a command button to the form and on the first dialog of the Command Button Wizard choose the Category: *Form Operations* and the Action: *Close Form.*

7   Click the Next button and give the button a text caption of &OK.

8   Click the Next button, name the button cmdOK and click the Finish button.

9   Caption the labels *&First Name(s)* and *&Last Name.*

We use First Name(s) rather than First Name because it is common to have Directors with names such as Stephen T. Kay. If the users began putting middle names into the *Last Name* field some of our future queries may not work as expected.

10   Set the *cmdOK* button's Default property to *Yes* so that users can dismiss the form by pressing the <Enter> key.

The finished form looks like this:

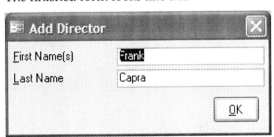

The form is useless in its present form. It will become useful when we invoke it in *Add mode* from the *frmFilm* form in the next lesson.

tip

Adjusting the display size of a dialog box form

If you have set the Border Style of a form to Dialog and you find you need to re-size it you'll need to do this in Design View.

Lesson 9-5: Add a command button to invoke the Add Director form

1 Open *frmFilm* in Design View.

2 Add a command button just to the right of the cboDirector combo box.

The first dialog of the Command Button Wizard appears.

3 Choose the Category:*Form Operations* and the Action:*Open Form* and click the Next button.

4 Choose frmAddDirector as the form to open and click the Next button.

5 Stay with the default *Open the form and show all the records* option. We will shortly change this using VBA code.

6 Give the command button a text caption of Add (we can't use a hotkey as there are no suitable letters left to use).

7 Name the button cmdShowAddDirectorForm and click the Finish button.

Your form should now look like this:

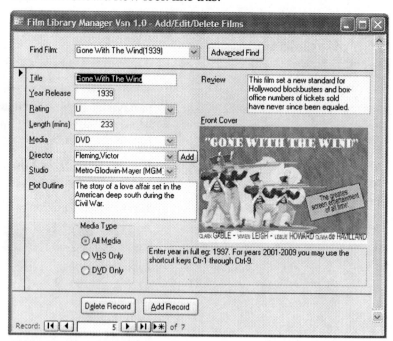

8 Make the form open in Add mode

Open the code for the cmdShowAddDirectorForm control's Click event.

Edit the following line of code:

```
Call DoCmd.OpenForm( stDocName, , , stLinkCriteria)
```

... so that it reads:

Session9d

```
Call DoCmd.OpenForm( stDocName, , , stLinkCriteria, _
acFormAdd, acDialog)
```

The new *acFormAdd* parameter tells the OpenForm method of the DoCmd object to open the form in *Add mode*.

The new *acDialog* parameter tells the OpenForm method that this is a modal dialog. This is essential for the requery code we're about to add to be successful (see sidebar).

9   Refresh the contents of cboDirector when returning from the frmAddDirector form and tidy the error handler.

Add the code:

```
Me.cboDirector.Requery
```

This will refresh the contents of the combo box after returning from the frmAddDirector form.

Cut and paste error handling code from another sub so that the code looks like this:

```
Private Sub cmdShowAddDirectorForm_Click()

On Error GoTo Err_cmdShowAddDirectorForm_Click

    Dim stDocName As String
    Dim stLinkCriteria As String

    stDocName = "frmAddDirector"
    DoCmd.OpenForm stDocName, , , stLinkCriteria, _
    acFormAdd, acDialog
    Me.cboDirector.Requery

    CleanUpAndExit:
    Exit Sub

Err_cmdShowAddDirectorForm_Click:
Call MsgBox("An error was encountered" & vbCrLf & _
    vbCrLf & _
    "Description: " & Err.Description & vbCrLf & _
    "Error Number: " & Err.Number, , "Error")
    Resume CleanUpAndExit

End Sub
```

Note that the wizard has created a completely redundant variable called *stLinkCriteria*. This could be used to set an SQL Where clause in order to filter the recordset underpinning the Add Director form. Even though it is redundant we won't bother removing it as it isn't doing any harm.

10   Test the command button.

Click the Add Record button and add a test record with the Film Name: *Goldfinger*. Because we do not have the director: *Guy Hamilton* click the Add button next to the Director combo box. The Add Director form is displayed.

Add the director *Guy Hamilton* and click the OK button.

11   Open the cboDirector control's drop down list. The director Guy Hamilton now appears in the list.

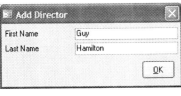

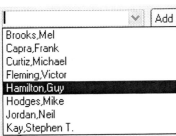

Lesson 9-6: Improve the code to auto-select the contents of the combo box

The pop-up frmAddDirector form works reasonably well but it could be even better.

When a new director is added the cboDirector combo box remains empty upon returning to frmFilm. The user then has to manually select the newly added director.

In this lesson we'll improve the Add Director feature so that the cboDirector combo box on the frmFilm form is automatically set to the name of the added director prior to the frmAddDirector form closing.

This will involve invoking events and setting properties on the frmFilm form from the frmAddDirector form.

1 Open the code window to show the event handler for the cmdAddFilm command button's Click event on the frmFilm form.

2 Remove the following line of code form the event handler:

```
Me.cboDirector.Requery
```

The code is removed because we're going to requery the frmFilmform remotely from the frmAddDirector film.

3 Open the code window to show the event handler for the cmdOK command button's Click event on the frmAddDirector form.

4 Modify the code as follows:

```
Private Sub cmdOK_Click()

On Error GoTo Err_cmdOK_Click

Me.Refresh

With Forms!frmFilm.cboDirector
    .Requery
    .SetFocus
    .Text = Me.txtLastName & "," & Me.txtFirstName
End With
DoCmd.Close

Exit_cmdOK_Click:

    Exit Sub

Err_cmdOK_Click:

    MsgBox Err.Description
    Resume Exit_cmdOK_Click

End Sub
```

Session9e

How the code works:

`Me.Refresh`

The form's Refresh method immediately updates the records in the Director table. We can now be certain that the table physically contains the new record.

`.Requery`

Execute the SQL code that underpins the cboDirector combo box on the frmFilm form. Because we know that the table now has the new director details we also know that the new director now exists within the cboDirector combo box list.

`.SetFocus`

We need to set focus to the cboDirector combo box because Access will not allow us to update a control property unless that control has focus. We need to update a cboDirector property in the next line of code.

`.Text = Me.txtLastName & "," & Me.txtFirstName`

Because the newly added director must now be a valid entry for the cboDirector combo box we can set it's Text property to the newly added director's name.

`DoCmd.Close`

The form is closed and the user returned to frmFilm where the newly added director should be visible in the cboDirector combo box.

5   Test the combo box.

Open the frmFilm form, click the Add Record button and add a test record with the Film Name: *The Sound of Music*.

Because we do not have the director: *Robert Wise* click the Add button next to the Director combo box. The Add Director form is displayed.

Add the director *Robert Wise* and click the OK button.

You are returned to the frmFilm form and Robert Wise is already selected as the Director.

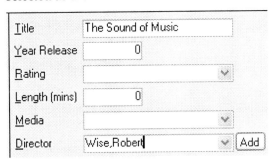

Lesson 9-7: Add simple forms to maintain static data

Users are now able to add new static data records from the frmFilm form and thus have a very streamlined and efficient way of quickly adding new film records—even where a new entry is required in the Media, Studio or Director static data tables.

The static data maintenance tools available to the user are still a little lacking as users have no means to delete or edit *Media, Studio, Director* or *Actor* details.

In this lesson we'll use the *Form Wizard* to create four simple static data maintenance forms.

1   Select the Form object and double-click *Create form by using wizard.*

2   Choose the Director table and select the DirectorFirstName and DirectorLastName fields but not the DirectorID field as it is meaningless and thus of no interest to the user.

3   Click the Next button and Accept the default *Columnar* layout.

4   Click the Next button and Accept the default *Standard* style.

5   Name the form frmMaintainDirector and click the Finish button.

6   Add an event handler to the new form's Load event and enter the following code:

```
Private Sub Form_Load()

Me.Caption = TSM_APPLICATION_NAME & _
                " - Maintain Directors"

End Sub
```

7   Use the same technique to create a maintenance form for the Media, Studio and Actor tables. When you have finished the forms should look like the following:

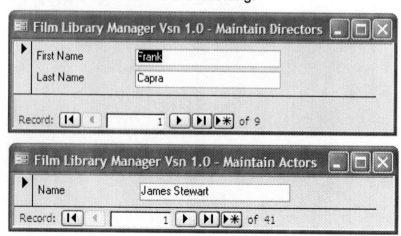

Session9f

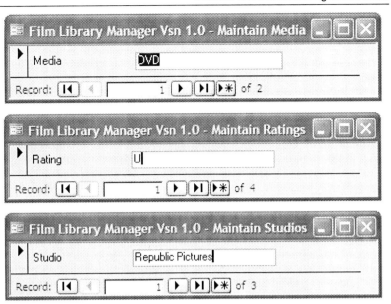

In a later session we'll provide the user with easy access to these forms from a drop-down menu driven user interface.

8   Use the command button wizard to add a delete button to each form.

This will be needed later as we will remove the shortcut menus and delete button on the toolbar when we finalise the application for deployment.

Without a delete button the user would be unable to delete static data records.

Session 9: Exercise

1   Create a new blank database named *Exercise9*.

2   Create a new form named *frmTest* and set its *RecordSelectors, Navigation Buttons* and *Dividing Lines* properties to *No*.

3   Add a command button to the form dismissing the Wizard if it appears.

4   Set the new command button's Caption property to: *&Close* and name it appropriately.

5   Add a new code module called *Utility Functions*.

6   Create a sub in the *Utility Functions* module called *CloseForm* that will accept a single string argument of *strFormName* and will then prompt the user with the message:

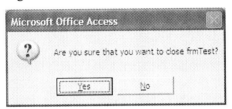

If the user clicks the *Yes* button the function will then call the *DoCmd* object's *CloseForm* method to close the form name requested. If you have difficulty coding this function slide the page slightly to the left to view the Q5 code listing.

7   Create a globally visible string constant in the Utility Functions module called TSM_APPLICATION_NAME and set the constant to the value "Session 9 Exercise"

If you have difficulty coding this function slide the page slightly to the left to view the Q6 code listing.

8   Add code to the frmTest form's *Load* event that will replace the form's caption property with the contents of the TSM_APPLICATION_NAME constant.

If you have difficulty coding this function slide the page slightly to the left to view the Q7 code listing.

9   Add some code to the *cmdCloseForm* control's Click event handler that will call the recently created *CloseForm* utility function passing the name of the form as an argument.

If you have difficulty coding this function slide the page slightly to the left to view the Q8 code listing

10   Test the form.

Open *frmTest* and note the caption. It should be: *Session 9 Exercise*. Click the cmdCloseForm command button. The confirmation dialog should appear. Test both the Yes and No buttons.

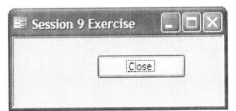 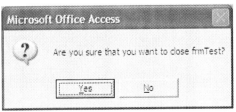

Exercise9

Session 9: Exercise answers

Q8	Q7	Q6	Q5

```
Private Sub cmdClose_Click()
Call CloseForm("frmTest")
End Sub
```

```
Private Sub Form_Load()
Me.Caption = TSM_APPLICATION_NAME
End Sub
```

```
Public Const TSM_APPLICATION_NAME As String = "Session 9 Exercise"
```

```
Public Sub CloseForm(strFormName As String)

Dim mbxResponse As VbMsgBoxResult

mbxResponse = MsgBox("Are you sure that you want to close " & _
strFormName & "?", vbQuestion + vbYesNo)

If mbxResponse = vbYes Then
    Call DoCmd.Close(acForm, strFormName)
End If

End Sub
```

Session Ten: Validations and Sub-Forms

> The longer I live the more I see that I am never wrong about anything, and that all the pains I have so humbly taken to verify my notions have only wasted my time.
>
> *George Bernard Shaw, Irish dramatist & socialist (1856 - 1950)*

In an ideal world all data entry personnel would be just like George Bernard Shaw and never make any mistakes. Unfortunately the world is not ideal and we have to give users of our forms a little help by validating their input.

It is easy to add simple validation to individual form fields without using VBA. As business rules become more complex it may not be possible to implement the required logic without hand-crafting the validation rules in VBA. In this session we're going to add some sophisticated VBA validation rules to our form.

Most Access developers will be familiar with adding a subform to show and update records on the many side of a one-to-many relationship but find themselves struggling when building a user interface to maintain data within a many-to-many relationship. We have such a relationship in our database:

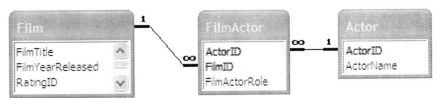

One Film has many Actors (each having a Role) and one Actor may appear in many different Films.

Our users want to be able to quickly associate an Actor with a Film (stating the Actor's *Role* in the film) and also want to be able to quickly add new actors to the Actor table.

Session Objectives

By the end of this session you will be able to:

- Add an advisory validation using VBA code
- Add a VBA table-level business rule to a form
- Create a sub form with self updating combo box
- Add a sub form to a form

Session10

Lesson 10-1: Add an advisory validation

Without resorting to code it is only possible to implement a mandatory validation rule. Often you will want to advise users of a possible error but allow them to continue when they feel that a special case exists where the validation rule may be safely broken.

With few exceptions films do not last more than 250 minutes. *Gone With The Wind* at 233 minutes was probably the longest mainstream film ever released.

There are some notable exceptions to the 250 minute rule. For example, Andy Warhol released a film in 1967 that lasted 25 hours. It would be wrong to prohibit the addition of such a film to the database.

We need to implement a rule that will warn the user when a film seems too long but will allow users to over-ride the warning when they are sure that the length is correct.

1   Add an event handler for the frmFilm form's BeforeUpdate event.

The *BeforeUpdate* event triggers before any data is written to the database. This is clearly the right place for any validation code. The *Cancel* argument of the BeforeUpdate event allows cancellation of the database update to be signalled in code.

2   Add the following code to the event handler:

```
Private Sub Form_BeforeUpdate(Cancel As Integer)

Dim mbxResult As VbMsgBoxResult

If Me.txtFilmLengthMinutes.value > 250 Then
    mbxResult = MsgBox("Film length is over " & _
    "250 minutes. Is this correct?", _
    vbQuestion + vbOKCancel)
End If

If mbxResult = vbCancel Then
    Cancel = True
    Me.txtFilmLengthMinutes.SetFocus
End If

End Sub
```

The code tests the current value in the txtFilmLengthMinutes text box control.

If the value is greater than 250 it asks the user whether the value is correct.

The MsgBox function returns a special data type (vbMsgBoxResult). If this data type has the value vbCancel (a built-in VB constant variable) the update is cancelled and focus is set to the txtFilmLengthMinutes control ready for the user to correct the error.

Session10

3   Test the form.

Click the Add Record button and title the new film *Test film*. You must enter a Title because it has been defined as a required field within the table properties.

Enter a value of 300 for the film's length and then click the Add Record button again to save the record. The error message is displayed.

Test both the case of adding the record (by clicking the OK button) and the case where the user wishes to correct the entry (by pressing the Cancel button).

Note that when the user cancels the entry focus is set to the txtFilmLengthMinutes text box.

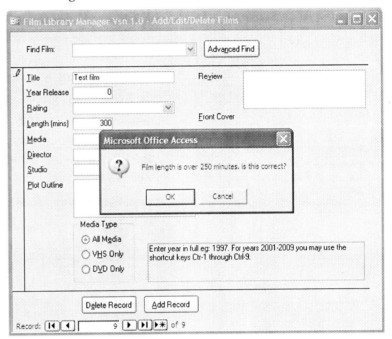

Lesson 10-2: Add a VBA business rule to a form

As the database currently stands it is easily possible to add duplicate director records. This is something we would like to prevent.

1   Prevent the user from closing the frmAddDirector form using the control box.

Set the frmAddDirector form's *Control Box* property to *No*.

2   Add a Cancel button to the frmAddDirector form.

Dismiss the Command Button Wizard if it appears. Set the command button's Caption property to *&Cancel* and name it *cmdCancel*.

3   Code the cmdCancel button's Click event.

When the user clicks the Cancel button the form must close without saving changes.

If the form is closed using the DoCmd object's Close method the record will automatically save its contents. To prevent this we need to invoke the form's *Undo* method prior to closing it.

Add the following code to the event handler:

```
Private Sub cmdCancel_Click()
    Me.Undo
    Call DoCmd.Close
End Sub
```

4   Locate the event handler for the cmdOK button's Click event on the frmAddDirector form.

We already have code in this event that will save the new director to the table. Code will be added here to make sure that the director does not exist prior to the save.

5   Obtain a reference to the cboDirector recordset.

Add the following two lines of code (shown boldface) to the event handler:

```
Private Sub cmdOK_Click()

On Error GoTo Err_cmdOK_Click

Dim rs As DAO.Recordset
Set rs = Forms!frmFilm.cboDirector.Recordset
```

You now have a reference to the recordset that underpins the cboDirector combo box on the frmFilm form.

6   Search the combo box recordset to see whether the director we are proposing to add already exists.

You may recall that the SQL query underpinning this combo box concatenates the Director's name with a separating comma and gives the new calculated field the name *Director*.

Session10a

We need to concatenate the contents of the two text boxes: *txtDirectorFirstName* and *txtDirectorLastName* and then use the recordset's *FindFirst* method to see whether the Director is already present in the table.

Add the following code to the event handler:

```
Call rs.FindFirst("Director = '" & _
Me.txtDirectorLastName.Value & _
"," & Me.txtDirectorFirstName.Value & "'")
```

7   Cause the update to fail if the director already exists.

Add the following code to the event handler:

```
If rs.NoMatch = False Then
    Call MsgBox("This director has already been added")
```

The above code will display the message box if the Director proposed for addition already exists.

8   Use the IF...Else...End if construct to only update when the Director does not already exist.

Further modify the event handler's code so that it reads as follows:

```
Private Sub cmdOK_Click()

On Error GoTo Err_cmdOK_Click

Dim rs As DAO.Recordset
Set rs = Forms!frmFilm.cboDirector.Recordset

Call rs.FindFirst("Director = '" & _
Me.txtDirectorLastName.Value & _
"," & Me.txtDirectorFirstName.Value & "'")

If rs.NoMatch = True Then
    Me.Refresh
    Forms!frmFilm.cboDirector.Requery
    Forms!frmFilm.cboDirector.SetFocus

    Forms!frmFilm.cboDirector.Text = _
    Me.txtDirectorLastName.Value & "," & _
    Me.txtDirectorFirstName.Value

    DoCmd.Close
Else
    Call MsgBox("This director has already been added")
End If

Exit_cmdOK_Click:
    Exit Sub

Err_cmdOK_Click:
    MsgBox Err.Description
    Resume Exit_cmdOK_Click
End Sub
```

9   Test the form.

It should no longer be possible to add a duplicate director name.

Session10b

Lesson 10-3: Design a query for the many-to-many subform

In order to give you an insight into how to specify applications we've prepared a mini functional and user-interface specification for the many-to-many subform. See sidebar for more details.

Many-to-many subform functional specification

■ The user will be able to quickly associate actors with films and to record their roles without leaving the main Add/Edit/Delete Films form.

■ The user will be able to add new actors without leaving the main Add/Edit/Delete Films form.

■ Actors will be listed in alphabetical order.

User interface specification

■ A subform will be provided on the main Add/Edit/Delete Films form.

■ The subform will have a self-updating drop-down combo control to allow actors to be associated with films and to allow new actors to be added.

■ The subform will have a text box so that the Actor's role can be entered.

Designing a query based upon this specification

The subform will require a FilmID in order to create a relationship between the FilmActor and Film tables.

The subform will require the ActorID field. Because this will be defined as a lookup field, a wizard generated form will implement this field as a normal (but not self-updating) combo box.

The FilmActorRole field will be required in order to allow the user to enter the Role.

In order to alphabetically sort by *FilmTitle* and *ActorName* we'll also need the *ActorName* and *FilmTitle* fields from the Film and Actor tables (see sidebar: *Using lookup fields in queries*).

1   Click the Queries object in the Database window.

2   Double-click *Create query in Design View*.

3   Add the Film, Actor and FilmActor tables to the query design window.

4   Drag the following fields into the grid:

Table	Fields
Film	FilmTitle
FilmActor	FilmID
FilmActor	ActorID
FilmActor	FilmActorRole
Actor	ActorName

note

Using Lookup fields in queries

Earlier we stated that Lookup fields can confuse novice developers but for the experienced Access developer they are very useful in jump-starting prototype form development.

This is one of those cases where it is necessary to understand the inner workings of Lookup fields in order to correctly design the query.

At first glance you might think that you do not need the *FilmTitle* field from the *Film* table or the *ActorName* field from the *Actor* table. The query result displays the textual *FilmTitle* and *ActorName* in the *FilmID* and *ActorID* fields so why not just use these for the sort?

It is important to realise that we can't use a Lookup field result to set a sort or criteria as we'd be applying this to the actual field content (the numeric primary keys) and not to the values displayed by Access (via the Lookup feature).

The values displayed in the query result by Access are simply a user interface feature and mask the true contents of the fields returned by the query that underpins the form.

5 Alphabetically sort by *Film Title* and then *Actor Name* ascending.

6 Set the ActorName and FilmTitle fields so that they do not show in the query result by clearing their *Show* check box.

Your query should now look like this:

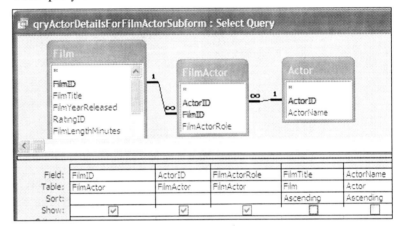

7 Test run the query.

Films are shown in alphabetical order with the Actors (in alphabetical order for each film) and their Roles alongside.

Film	Actor	Role
Blazing Saddles	Alex Karras	Mongo
Blazing Saddles	Cleavon Little	Bart
Blazing Saddles	David Huddleston	Olsen Johnson
Blazing Saddles	Gene Wilder	Jim (The Waco Kid)
Blazing Saddles	Liam Dunn	Rev Jackson
Blazing Saddles	Slim Pickens	Taggart
Casablanca	Claude Rains	Capt. Renault
Casablanca	Conrad Veidt	Maj. Strasser
Casablanca	Humphrey Bogart	Rick Blaine

8 Save the query with the name *qryActorDetailsForFilmActorSubform*.

Lesson 10-4: Create the many-to-many subform

Now that the subform query has been designed we can use it as a basis for our subform.

While the subform wizard is a convenient way to automatically create simple one-to-many subforms it is a better to take a two-step approach.

First we'll design the subform and then add some more advanced features in the next session.

Only when the subform is ready to use will it be linked in to the frmFilm form using the wizard.

1   Click the Forms object in the Database window.

2   Double-click *Create form by using wizard.*

The first dialog of the Form Wizard appears.

3   Choose qryActorDetailsForFilmActorSubform as the data source for the form.

4   Select all three fields from the query result.

5   Click the Next button twice to select the default Columnar report type and Standard style.

6   Name the form frmFilmActorSubform and click the Finish button.

The subform is displayed.

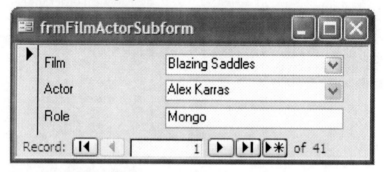

7   Change the frmFilmActorSubform form's *Default View* property to *Datasheet.*

8   Switch to Form View.

The form is shown in Datasheet view. This is how the form will appear when embedded within the frmFilm form as a subform.

Session10c

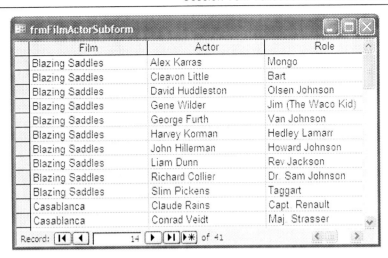

9   Drag the right-hand side of the Film column header to the far left of the screen to hide it.

The column headed *Film* is actually the FilmID field. It is displaying the FilmTitle due to our previously defining this field as a lookup field.

We want to hide the Film Title because this form is destined to become a sub-form within frmFilm and the film title will already be displayed on the main frmFilm form.

10   Rename the Actor combo box from ActorID to cboActor.

The Actor field in our subform has been automatically named Actor by the wizard. Because this violates our naming convention it should be correctly named as cboActor (return to Design View and change the *Name* property of the combo box to *cboActor*).

11   Test the subform.

The subform now displays only the Actor and Role fields. It is possible to change the actor associated with a Role using a drop-down combo list.

The combo list isn't yet self-updating. We'll be converting this in the next lesson.

Lesson 10-5: Convert the combo box to self-updating

The subform is now almost ready to be added to the main frmFilm form. Before it is added we need to convert the Actor combo box to a self-updating combo box so that the user can quickly add new actors without leaving the main form.

The code for the self-updating combo box is almost the same as for the self-updating combo boxes on the *frmFilm* form. You can simply cut-and paste it from one of the existing *NotInList* event handlers and then make the required small changes.

1   Convert the Actor combo box to a self-updating combo box using the techniques learned in the earlier session by adding the following code to its NotInList event:

```
Private Sub cboActor_NotInList(NewData As String,
Response As Integer)

Dim mbxResponse As VbMsgBoxResult
Dim strActor As String
Dim strSQL As String

mbxResponse = MsgBox("Are you sure you want to add " &
NewData & _
" as a valid actor?", vbQuestion + vbYesNo)

If mbxResponse = vbYes Then

    NewData = SQLSafe(NewData)

    strSQL = "INSERT INTO Actor([ActorName]) " & _
             "VALUES ('" & NewData & "');"

    DoCmd.SetWarnings False
    DoCmd.RunSQL strSQL
    DoCmd.SetWarnings True

    MsgBox "The new actor has been added to the list." _
        , vbInformation

    Response = acDataErrAdded

Else

    Response = acDataErrDisplay

End If
```

1   Test the form:

Add a new actor by directly typing the actor name into one of the Actor fields.

Session10d

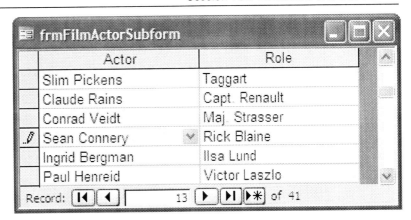

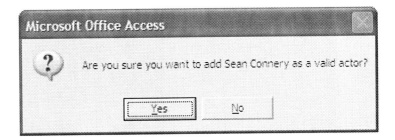

The form is now exactly what is needed and can be incorporated into the frmFilm form in the next lesson.

Lesson 10-6: Add a subform

1   Open frmFilm in Design View.

2   Make the form a lot wider and then place a Subform/Subreport control onto the right hand side of the form.

     The first screen of the Subform Wizard is displayed.

3   Choose the option *Use an existing form* and select the frmFilmActorSubform.

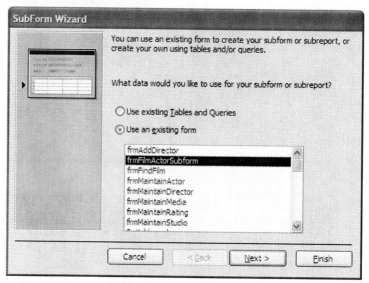

4   Click the Next button.

     Choose the option *Define my own* and choose the FilmID field in both boxes to define the Primary Key/Foreign Key relationship between the forms.

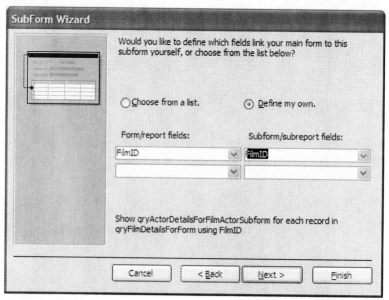

5   Click the Next button and name the subform *Actors:*

6   Click the Finish button and re-size the control so that it fills the right hand side of the form.

Session10e

7   Your form should now look like this:

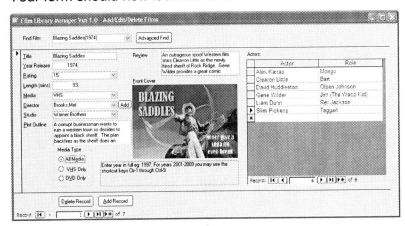

8   Test the form

In the film Blazing Saddles (1974) other members of the cast
included:

Actor	Role
John Hillerman	Howard Johnson
George Furth	Van Johnson
Harvey Korman	Hedley Lamarr
Richard Collier	Dr. Sam Johnson

Use the improved form to add the four actors and record their role
in the film.

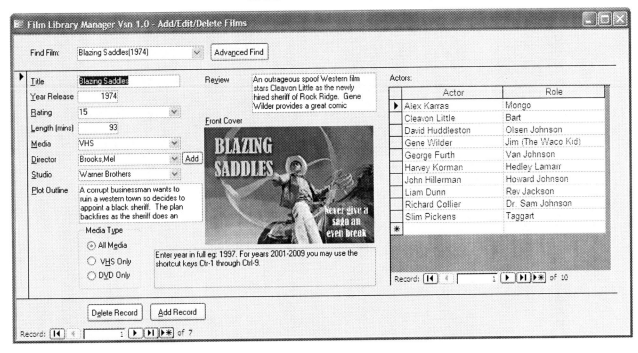

Session 10: Exercise

1   Create a new blank database named *Exercise10*.

2   Create the following three tables

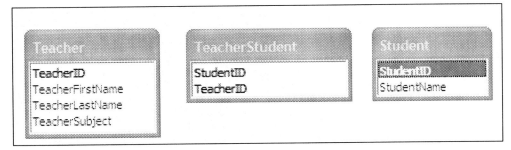

The tables will model the many-to-many relationship:

One Teacher has many Students and one Student has many Teachers.

Do not set any relationships yet but do set appropriate data types, captions and primary keys. If you have any difficulty constructing the tables you can view the Q2 answer overleaf.

3   **Set the StudentID and TeacherID fields in the TeacherStudent table to be Lookup fields referencing the Student and Teacher tables.**

4   Use the Form Wizard to create a form named *frmTeacher* that will maintain *Teacher* records and a form named frmStudent that will maintain Student records.

5   Use the new forms to add three teacher records and ten student records (make up some names).

6   Use the form wizard to create a new form called TeacherStudentSubform. Be sure to include both TeacherID and StudentID fields. Change the default view to Datasheet View and make sure that the TeacherID field is re-sized to zero width to hide it from view.

7   Make the frmTeacher form larger and add the frmTeacherStudentSubform to it so that students may be associated with teachers.

8   Change the caption of the Teacher form to Teachers and Students.

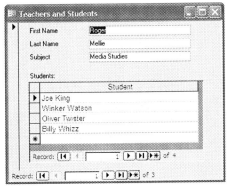

Exercise10

Session 10: Exercise answers

Q2 The three tables should be constructed with the following Fields, Data Types and Captions:

Table	Field	Data Type	Caption
Student	StudentID	AutoNumber (PK)	
	StudentName	Text	Name
Teacher	TeacherID	AutoNumber (PK)	
	TeacherFirstName	Text	First Name
	TeacherLastName	Text	Last Name
	TeacherSubject	Text	Subject
TeacherStudent	StudentID	Lookup (PK)	Student
	TeacherID	Lookup (PK)	Teacher

Note that the *TeacherStudent* Many-to-Many link table has a concatenated primary key made up of the Foreign keys from the tables on either side of the relationship.

The sample file *Exercise10* available for download from our web site contains the completed database. Study this and the text of the preceding session if you have any difficulties building this application.

Note that in a real-world application you'd also change the relationship properties to enforce referential integrity as you wouldn't want it to be possible to delete a teacher that was associated with students.

This is also one of the cases where you might consider allowing a cascading delete between the *Teacher* and *TeacherStudent* tables so that the deletion of a teacher automatically deleted any relationship between the teacher and students.

Session Eleven: Creating a Dialog-Driven Report

> Don't reinvent the wheel, just realign it.
>
> *Anthony J. D'Angelo, The College Blue Book*

Often users will request a suite of reports that are all variations of one generic report type. In an Access application written without VBA it is possible to create simple report parameters by basing the report upon a parameter-driven query but it is not possible to create sophisticated dialog-driven reports specifying complex filter conditions.

In this session we will drive two reports from the same dialog box which will enable the user to both choose the report and to specify a filter condition. The dialog will be kept simple but the skills learned will enable you to create sophisticated dialogs that will cater for any user-specified filtering need.

You'll find that once you are able to data-drive your reports you will often be able to substitute one dialog-driven report for several single-purpose reports. This will empower you to avoid reinventing the wheel!

Session Objectives

By the end of this session you will be able to:

- Create and format a report
- Use a tab control
- Use a dialog box to gather and set report parameters

Session11

Lesson 11-1: Design a query for the report

1   Make a copy of the qryFilmDetails query and rename it qryFilmDetailsForFilmCatalogue.

Right-click the qryFilmDetails query in the query window and choose Copy. Right-click again and choose Paste to copy the query. Right-click the copied query and choose Rename to rename the query.

2   Open the query in Design View.

At the moment the query will return all film details but does not return any actor records.

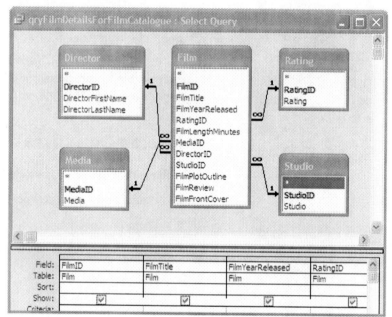

3   Add the Actor and FilmActor tables to the query designer and set the join properties.

Click the Show Table Button to add the two new tables.

Right-click on the join between the Film and FilmActor tables and select the second option: *Include ALL records from 'Film' and only those records from 'FilmActor' where the joined fields are equal.*

This is called a *left* join. The last option would produce a *right* join.

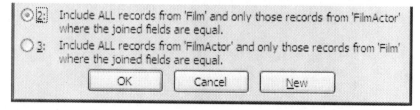

If the join were left at default (a join type called an inner-join or equi-join) any film record that had no actor details entered would not be shown in the query result.

Session11

Do the same for the join between the FilmActor and Actor tables. This time you will choose the third option: *Include ALL records from 'FilmActor' and only those records from 'Actor' where the joined fields are equal.*

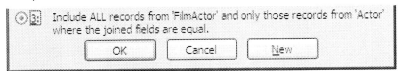

4   The query designer now shows the joins between the tables with an arrow on the end of each join indicating that all Film records will be shown regardless of whether a matching Actor, Rating, Studio, Director or Media record exists.

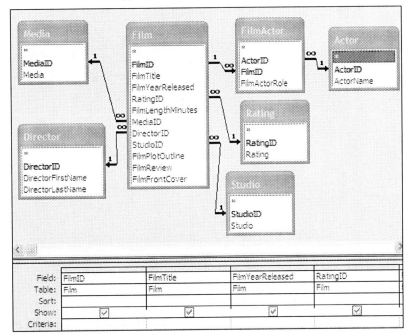

Field:	FilmID	FilmTitle	FilmYearReleased	RatingID
Table:	Film	Film	Film	Film
Sort:				
Show:	☑	☑	☑	☑
Criteria:				

5   Add the FilmActorRole field from the FilmActor table and the ActorName field from the Actor table to the query.

We're going to list all actors and their roles in the Film Catalogue report so will need these fields available within the query.

6   Add an alphabetical sort so that results are sorted first by FilmTitle and then by ActorName.

7   Test run the query.

Note that the alphabetical sort by film title and actor is working correctly.

FilmTitleAndYear	Name	Role
Blazing Saddles(1974)	Alex Karras	Mongo
Blazing Saddles(1974)	Cleavon Little	Bart
Blazing Saddles(1974)	David Huddleston	Olsen Johnson
Blazing Saddles(1974)	Gene Wilder	Jim (The Waco Kid)
Blazing Saddles(1974)	George Furth	Van Johnson
Blazing Saddles(1974)	Harvey Korman	Hedley Lamarr
Blazing Saddles(1974)	John Hillerman	Howard Johnson
Blazing Saddles(1974)	Liam Dunn	Rev Jackson
Blazing Saddles(1974)	Richard Collier	Dr. Sam Johnson
Blazing Saddles(1974)	Slim Pickens	Taggart
Casablanca(1942)	Claude Rains	Capt. Renault

Lesson 11-2: Create the prototype report

1 Click the Reports object in the Database window.

2 Double click *Create report by using wizard.*

The first dialog of the Report Wizard opens.

3 Use qryFilmDetailsForFilmCatalogue as the query that will underpin the report.

4 Select the following fields (in the order shown) for the new report.

5 Click the Next button and choose to view *By Film*.

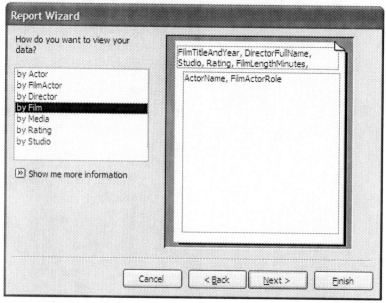

6 Click the Next button twice as we do not want to create any grouping levels.

7 Click the Next button again as the sort order we want has already been defined within the query.

Session11a

8   Select the *Align Left 1* layout, stay with the default *Portrait* orientation and click the *Next* button.

9   Choose the *Formal* style and click the Next button.

10   Title the report *rptFilmCatalogue* and click the Finish button.

The prototype form is displayed. It isn't very pretty (or even useable) in its present state but the wizard has done a fine job of selecting all of the fields we need and has created appropriate report controls to provide a starting point.

In the next lessons we'll convert this into a useful and attractive report.

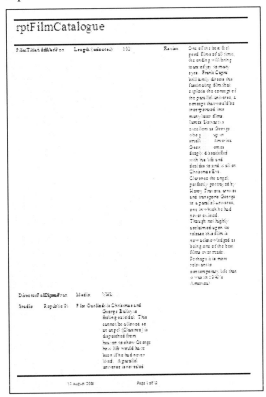

Lesson 11-3: Format the prototype report – first fix

1   Open rptFilmCatalogue in Design View.

2   Click the *Sorting and Grouping* button 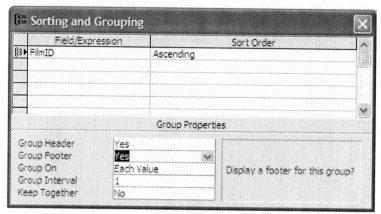 on the *Report Design* toolbar and add a *Group Footer* to the report.

Select the *FilmID* field at the top of the dialog and change the *Group Footer* property to *Yes*.

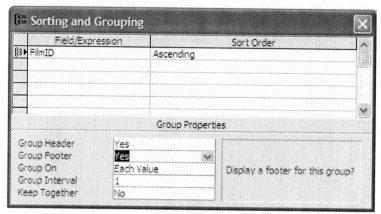

By adding a group footer we gain an area to place information from the Film table after we have listed the actors who took part in the film.

3   Move the *Review* label and *FilmReview* field to the new FilmID Footer report section.

4   Move the *Review* label and *FilmReview* field to the new *FilmID Footer* report section.

Increase the width of the FilmReview field so that it spans the entire page.

5   Reduce the size of the PageHeader report section to nothing by dragging the top of the *FilmID Header* gray dividing bar upwards until it touches the *PageHeader* gray dividing bar.

6   Arrange the fields in the *FilmID Header* report section to match the following:

Session11b

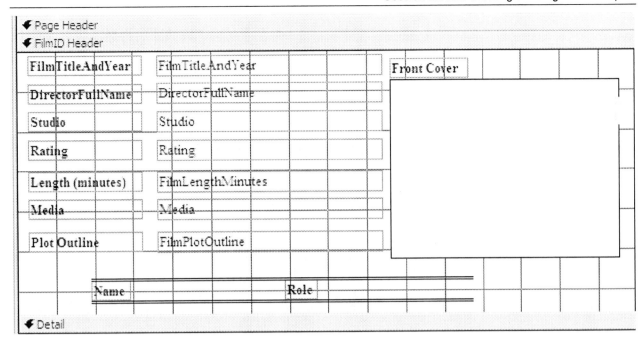

7   Test the report by viewing it in Print Preview view. It isn't perfect yet but it is closer to what is needed.

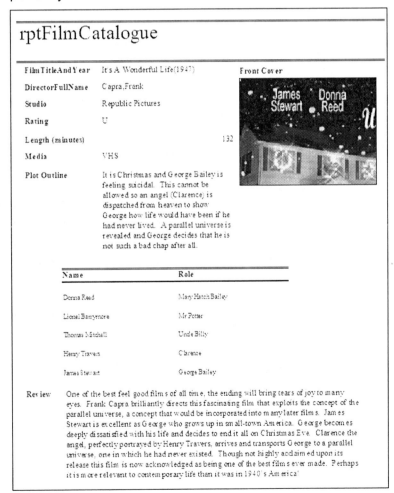

Lesson 11-4: Format the prototype report – second fix

note

Report design screen grab

The report in its finished state (after the second fix) is shown on the two pages that follow this lesson both in *Design View* and *Preview View*.

note

Finding image files (clipart)

Graphics bring alive applications and make them appear more professional.

There's a wealth of sources for clipart on the Web and extensive clipart collections bundled with other Office applications such as Word and PowerPoint.

A search on the web for the word: *ClipArt* produced over 56 million results so there is plenty to choose from! Make sure that your image is royalty-free (or purchase a licence to use it) if you intend to distribute it as part of a commercial application.

When you find a suitable image simply right-click on it in your web browser and choose *Save Picture As...* from the shortcut menu.

Google Images is another great web resource for clipart. A search for *"Film Icon"* produced many images that would be perfect for the Switchboard form.

1 Open rptFilmCatalogue in Design View.

2 Change the *Caption* property of the report from *rptFilmCatalogue* to *Film Catalogue*.

3 Change the caption of the label control in the Report Header section from *rptFilmCatalogue* to Film Catalogue.

4 Change the font of the new title to *Times New Roman 28 point bold italic*.

5 Make the *Title* label control a lot wider, so that it spans the entire width of the page and set the control's *Text Align* property to *Center*.

6 Make the page header report section a little larger by dragging the top of the Page Header gray dividing bar downwards.

7 Add a Page Break control at the bottom of the Page Header section.

8 Optionally add a suitable clip art graphic (see sidebar) into a picture control above the report title and some descriptive text in a label control or controls beneath the title.

9 Add a Page Break control at the bottom of the Page Header section.

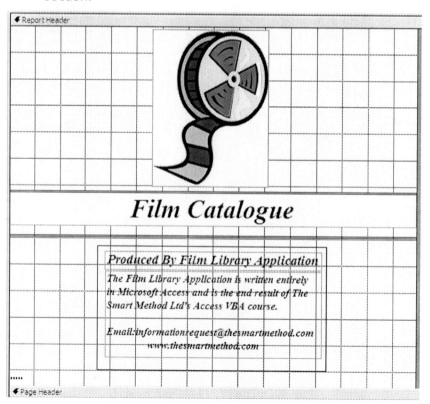

note

Choosing fonts

The first important rule is that you should never use more than two fonts in your reports. It is usually more effective to use a sans-serif font for headers and a serifed font for body text.

In our sample report we've used just one font: Times New Roman but it could have been effective to have used a sans-serif font for the name of the film at the top of each page.

Times New Roman was commissioned by The Times (London) newspaper in 1931 with a design brief to be the most readable typeface ever created. It remains the most popular serifed typeface in the world so is a great choice for your serifed font.

Helvetica is the name of a widely used sans-serif typeface developed in 1957 by Swiss graphic designer Max Miedinger and is probably the most widely used sans-serif font in the world. Microsoft's Arial font is virtually identical to Helvetica.

If you use nothing but Times New Roman and Arial your reports will always look professional!

note

Choosing margin sizes

The ruler should show 160mm of available white space in Design View. Because we are outputting to A4 paper which is 210mm wide the left and right margins must be exactly 25mm or we risk outputting a blank page between each report page.

The bottom margin is set to 10mm as we are using a report footer which will look odd if set to the same margin as the page header.

10 Align the *Actor* and *Role* text box controls and associated labels so that the controls are aligned with the fields above.

Select the *ActorName* text box, *Actor label* control, both *Line* controls and the *Plot Outline:* label above them and choose Format→Align→Left from the main menu.

11 Set the font size for the *ActorName* and *FilmActorRole* text boxes to 10 point to match the rest of the report.

12 Place the *Review* label above the *FilmReview* text box control and align both so that they are aligned with the ActorName text box.

13 Set the *FilmLengthMinutes* text box control's *TextAlign* property to *Left*.

14 Change the *FilmFrontCover* Bound Object Frame control's *Size Mode* property to *Zoom* and its *BorderStyle* property to *Transparent*.

15 Delete the label with the caption *FilmTitleAndYear*. Align the *FilmTitleAndYear* text box with the label controls beneath and widen it to span the entire width of the report.

16 Set the font of the FilmTitleAndYear text box to Times New Roman,14 Point, Bold.

17 Change the label control with the caption: *DirectorFullName* so that the caption is simply *Director*.

18 Remove the Text Box control containing *Now()* from the *Page Footer* section.

19 Re-size the remaining field in the PageFooter section (the one containing page number information) and set its *Text Align* property to *Center*.

20 Set appropriate margins.

Choose File→Page Setup from the main menu and set the Bottom margin to 10mm. Set the Left, Right and Top margins to 25mm.

21 Suppress the page footer for the Report Header page.

Set the Report's *Page Footer* property to *Not with Rpt Hdr*. This will cause the footer to be suppressed on the cover pages.

22 If any part of the report does not appear pleasing on the eye move, align and re-size controls until the report is attractive and professional looking.

23 Set the report's *Auto Center* property to *Yes*.

The report will now always display in the very center of the screen.

View the sample report and layout on the following two pages to see one possible way of making small adjustments to your finished report. Feel free to improve upon the report's appearance if it is not to your own taste.

Sample report Design View

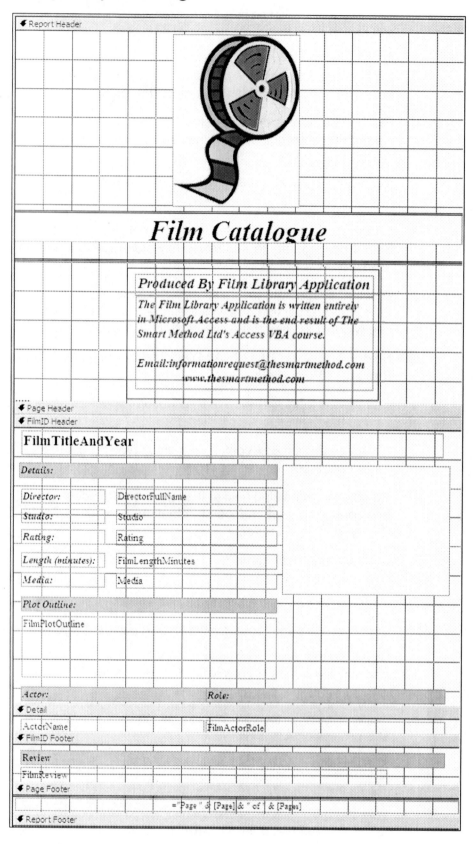

Sample report Print Preview view

It's A Wonderful Life(1947)

Details:

Director:	Capra,Frank
Studio:	Republic Pictures
Rating:	U
Length (minutes):	132
Media:	VHS

Plot Outline:

It is Christmas and George Bailey is feeling suicidal. This cannot be allowed so an angel (Clarence) is dispatched from heaven to show George how life would have been if he had never lived. A parallel universe is revealed and George decides that he is not such a bad chap after all.

Actor:	*Role:*
Donna Reed	Mary Hatch Bailey
Lionel Barrymore	Mr Potter
Thomas Mitchell	Uncle Billy
Henry Travers	Clarence
James Stewart	George Bailey

Review

One of the best feel good films of all time, the ending will bring tears of joy to many eyes. Frank Capra brilliantly directs this fascinating film that exploits the concept of the parallel universe, a concept that would be incorporated into many later films. James Stewart is excellent as George who grows up in small-town America. George becomes deeply dissatisfied with his life and decides to end it all on Christmas Eve. Clarence the angel, perfectly portrayed by Henry Travers, arrives and transports George to a parallel universe, one in which he had never existed. Though not highly acclaimed upon its release this film is now acknowledged as being one of the best films ever made. Perhaps it is more relevant to contemporary life than it was in 1940's America!

Lesson 11-5: Design the tab based user interface

Creating a dialog is a two-step process.

■ The user interface is designed first. No consideration is given at this stage to how the form will implement its functionality.

■ When the user interface is complete code is written to make the controls on the form actually work.

In this lesson we will consider only the first step—the user interface.

1 Select the Forms object in the Database window.

2 Double-click *Create form in Design View*.

3 Drop a Tab control onto the form.

4 Drop an *Option Group* control onto Page1 of the Tab control.

The first screen of the Option Group Wizard appears.

5 Set the *Label Names* to &All Media, &DVD Only and &VHS Only.

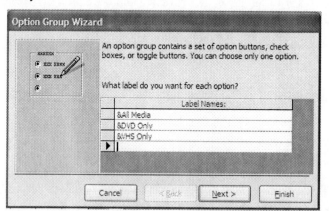

6 Click the Next button and leave the default choice set to &All Media.

7 Click the Next button three times to accept defaults and then set the Caption to &Filter.

8 Click the Finish button and change the Name property of the Option Group control to fraFilter.

Your Tab control should now look like this :

9 Right-click on the tab (currently captioned Page1) at the top of the Tab control, choose *Properties* from the shortcut

Session11d

menu, change the *Caption* property to *&Filter* and then close the properties dialog.

10 Right click on the tab (currently captioned Page2) at the top of the Tab control, choose Properties from the shortcut menu and change the Caption property to *&Report Type*.

The tabs should now look like this:

11 Drop an *Option Group* control onto the *Report Type* page of the tab control.

The first screen of the Option Group Wizard appears.

12 Set the Label Names to *Film &List (just one line per film)*, and *Full &Details*.

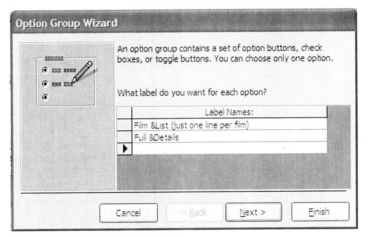

13 Click the Next button four times to accept default values and then set the option group caption to *&Report Type.*

14 Click the Finish button and change the Name property of the Option Group control to *fraReportType.* Re-size the Tab control so that there is little white space to the right of the option groups.

Your Tab control should now look like this:

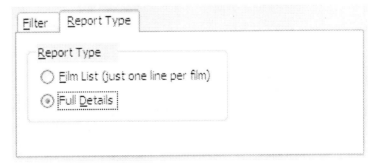

15 Save the form with the name *frmFilmReportCriteria.*

Lesson 11-6: Complete the user interface

1   Add three command button controls at the bottom of the form without using the wizard. Set the Caption properties to *&Cancel*, *&Print Catalogue* and *Previe&w Catalogue* and their Name properties to *cmdCancel*, *cmdPrintCatalogue* and *cmdPreviewCatalogue*.

2   Change the Caption property of the form to Report Criteria.

Your form should now look like this:

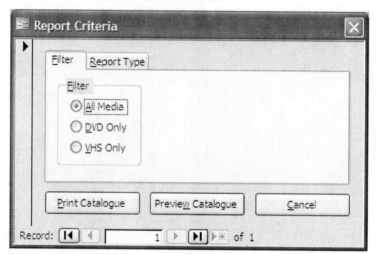

3   Convert the form to a popup modal dialog by setting the following properties:

Property	Value
Scroll Bars	Neither
Record Selectors	No
Navigation Buttons	No
Dividing Lines	No
Auto Center	Yes
Border Style	Dialog
Min Max Buttons	None
PopUp	Yes
Modal	Yes

Your form should now look like this:

Session11e

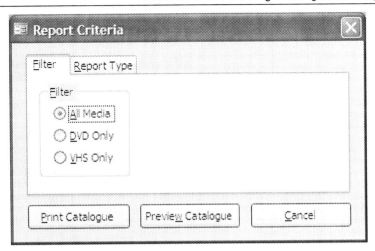

4   Add the following code to the Cancel command button's Click event.

```
Private Sub cmdCancel_Click()

DoCmd.Close

End Sub
```

5   Test the Cancel command button.

When the Cancel command button is clicked the form closes.

Lesson 11-7: Implement Print Preview functionality

1   Add the following code to the *Preview Catalogue* command button:

```
Private Sub cmdPreviewCatalogue_Click()
'Define variables
Dim strReportName As String
Dim strFilter As String

'Compute filter condition
If Me.fraFilter.Value = 2 Then ' DVD Only
    strFilter = "[Media] = 'DVD'"
ElseIf Me.fraFilter.Value = 3 Then ' VHS Only
    strFilter = "[Media] = 'VHS'"
Else ' All types and catch-all
    strFilter = ""
End If

'Determine report to run
If Me.fraReportType.Value = 1 Then ' Film List
    strReportName = "rptFilmList"
ElseIf Me.fraReportType.Value = 2 Then ' Full Details
    strReportName = "rptFilmCatalogue"
End If

' Run the report
Call DoCmd.OpenReport(strReportName, _
acViewPreview, , strFilter, acDialog)

' Close the dialog
Call DoCmd.Close(acForm, "frmReportCriteria")

End Sub
```

Define variables section

```
'Define variables
Dim strReportName As String
Dim strFilter As String
```

In this section two variables are defined with a data type of *String*. One will hold the report name as selected by the user in the *Report Type* tab of the dialog.

The other variable will hold an SQL filter condition that will be added as a WHERE clause to the SQL query underpinning the report.

Compute filter condition section

```
'Compute filter condition
If Me.fraFilter.Value = 2 Then ' DVD Only
    strFilter = "[Media] = 'DVD'"
ElseIf Me.fraFilter.Value = 3 Then ' VHS Only
    strFilter = "[Media] = 'VHS'"
```

Session11f

```
Else ' All types and catch-all
    strFilter = ""
End If
```

The goal of this section is to correctly set the strFilter variable with the SQL filter that matches the user's choice.

For example, if the user has chosen DVD the SQL filter would be :

[Media] = 'DVD'

… a valid SQL WHERE condition.

Determine report to run section

```
'Determine report to run
If Me.fraReportType.Value = 1 Then ' Film List
    strReportName = "rptFilmList"
ElseIf Me.fraReportType.Value = 2 Then ' Full Details
    strReportName = "rptFilmCatalogue"
End If
```

The goal of this section is to set the strReportName variable to the name of the report chosen by the user in the Report Type tab of the dialog.

Run the report section

```
' Run the report
Call DoCmd.OpenReport(strReportName, _
acViewPreview, , strFilter, acDialog)
```

The DoCmd object's *OpenReport* method is used to show the chosen report (stored in strReportName) in preview view (using the VBA built-in constant acViewPreview) with an SQL WHERE condition added to the underlying query as defined by the contents of the strFilter variable.

Note the use of the *acDialog* parameter to tell the report to preview as a dialog box. This will ensure that the report is at the front of the screen (floating above the frmFilm form).

Close the dialog section

```
' Close the dialog
Call DoCmd.Close(acForm, "frmReportCriteria")
```

The DoCmd object's *Close* method is used to close the frmReportCriteria dialog. Normally it would not be necessary to name the form to close, but in this case, the report has focus and simply calling the *Close* method without parameters would close the report that had just been opened rather than the dialog form.

Lesson 11-8: Implement Print functionality

1   Copy and paste the code from the cmdPreviewCatalogue button's *Click* event handler into the cmdPrintCatalogue button's *Click* event handler.

The code for the Print (rather than Print Preview) button is almost identical. All that is needed is to change the line:

```
Call DoCmd.OpenReport(strReportName, _
acViewPreview, , strFilter, acDialog)
```

To:

```
Call DoCmd.OpenReport(strReportName, _
acViewNormal, , strFilter, acDialog)
```

Changing the parameter from *acViewPreview* to *acViewNormal* will cause the report to be printed to hard copy rather than displayed on screen.

2   Open frmFilmReportCriteria in Form View and choose *DVD Only*.

The Report Criteria dialog is displayed:

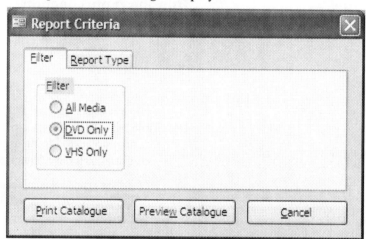

3   Click the *Report Type* tab and choose *Film List (just one line per film)*.

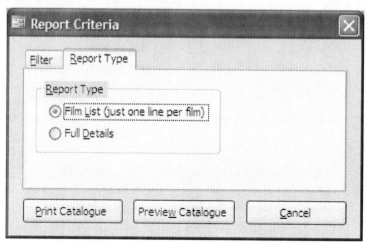

Session11g

4   Click the *Preview Catalogue* button.

The *rptFilmList* report is displayed showing only DVD movies.

5   Close the Film List report and choose *Full Details* as the report type.

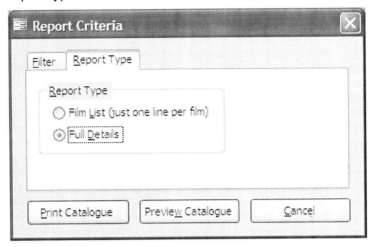

6   Click the *Preview Catalogue* button.

The *rptFilmCatalogue* report is displayed containing only DVD movies.

7   Test all other options.

Verify that the *rptFilmList* and *rptFilmCatalogue* reports also work as expected when the filter is set to *VHS* or *All Media*.

If you have a printer connected to your computer also confirm that the reports print out to hard copy as expected.

Session 11: Exercise

1   Make a copy of the FilmLibrary.mdb file and re-name it *Exercise11.mdb*.

2   Create a query that will return the *FilmTitle* and *FilmYearReleased* fields from the Film table along with the *Studio* field from the Studio table. Sort by *FilmTitle* ascending and *FilmYearReleased* ascending. Save this query with the name *qryFilmStudio*.

3   Run the query. The beginning of the result should be as follows:

Title	Year Released	Studio
Blazing Saddles	1974	Warner Brothers
Casablanca	1942	Warner Brothers
Get Carter	1971	Metro-Glodwin-Mayer (MGM)
Get Carter	2000	Warner Brothers
Gone With The Wind	1939	Metro-Glodwin-Mayer (MGM)

4   Use the report wizard to create a simple report based upon qryFilmStudio that will list the above three fields. Save the report with the name *rptFilmStudio*.

5   Create the following dialog form and save it with the name *frmFilmStudioCriteria*.

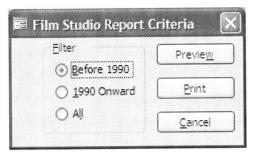

6   Add code to each of the three command buttons to make the form work.

7   Test the dialog form and report.

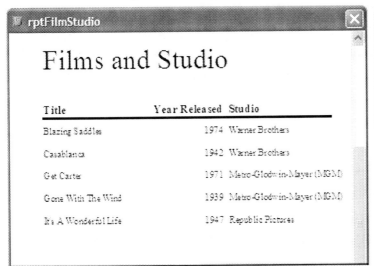

Exercise11

Session 11: Exercise answers

Q2   Construct the query as follows :

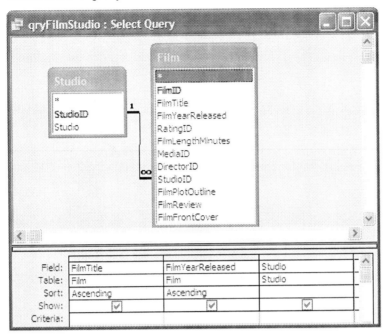

Q6   Use the following code in the command button event handlers:

```
Private Sub cmdCancel_Click()
DoCmd.Close
End Sub


Private Sub cmdPreview_Click()
' Define Variables
Dim strFilter As String

If Me.fraFilter.Value = 1 Then ' Before 1990
    strFilter = "[FilmYearReleased] < 1990"
ElseIf Me.fraFilter.Value = 2 Then ' 1990 Onward
    strFilter = "[FilmYearReleased] >= 1990"
Else ' All years and catch-all
    strFilter = ""
End If


' Run the report
Call DoCmd.OpenReport("rptFilmStudio", acViewPreview, , strFilter, acDialog)

' Close the dialog
Call DoCmd.Close(acForm, "frmFilmStudioCriteria")


End Sub
```

(The *cmdPrint_Click* event handler is programmed as *cmdPrintPreview_Click* but with the *acViewPreview* parameter changed to *acViewNormal*).

Session Twelve: Using Word with Access

An expert is a person who has made all the mistakes that can be made in a very narrow field.

Niels Bohr, Danish atomic physicist (1885—1962)

Access is a wonderful tool for storing and retrieving data. But Access is a little like Niels Bohr's experts—it is only good at what it is designed to do.

Word is also very good at what it is designed to do: Formatting and printing text and graphics to produce perfectly printed output.

Excel is the star of the desktop when it comes to analysing the data that Access is so good at storing and retrieving.

One of the most wonderful, and rarely exploited, features of the Office suite is the use of VBA code to mix and match features from all Office applications in order to produce custom-built applications that address specific needs.

We'll do just that in this session when we leverage upon Word's superb page layout capabilities to output film records as Word documents.

Session Objectives

By the end of this session you will be able to:

- Create a Word Document Template
- Create a command button that will open Word
- Transfer data from Access to Word

Session 12

Lesson 12-1: Create a Word document template

1   Open Word and create a document with the following text:

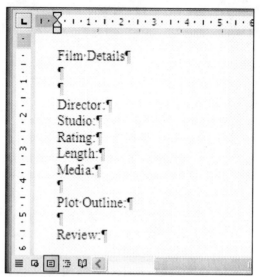

If the paragraph markers are not visible you will have to click the

Show/Hide button ¶ on the standard toolbar.

2   Select the text *Film Details* and the paragraph marker beneath it and change the font to *Arial Black 26 Points*.

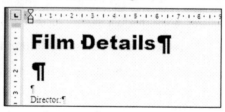

3   Select the remaining text and paragraph markers and change the font to Arial 12 Point Bold.

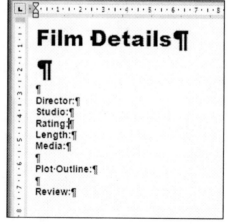

FilmDetails.dot

Session 12

4   Select the paragraph marker below *Film Details* and then select Insert→Bookmark from the main menu.

The Insert Bookmark dialog appears.

Type the name *bmkFilmTitle* in the Bookmark name box and click the *Add* button.

5   Place the insertion point just after the *Director:* text and press the <tab> key once, choose Insert→Bookmark once more and add a bookmark called *bmkFilmDirector*.

6   Do the same for Studio, Rating, Length, Media, Plot Outline and Review naming the bookmarks bmkStudio, bmkRating, bmkLength, bmkMedia, bmkPlotOutline and bmkReview but indent the last two items by two tabs.

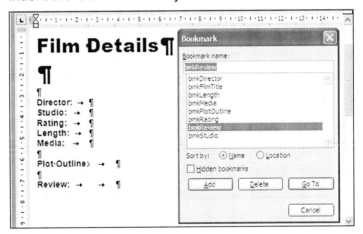

Select File→Save As … from the main menu and then select *Document Template* in the *Save as type:* drop down list and *Film Details* for the File name:

You have now saved a document template that we will be able to use in our Access VBA code to generate a nicely formatted Word document containing a single film record.

7   Close Word.

Lesson 12-2: Create a command button that will open Word

1   Open the frmFilm form in Design View and add a command button to the form.

The command button wizard is displayed.

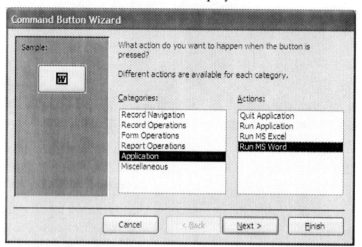

2   Choose the category:*Application* and action:*Run MS Word* from the Wizard's first dialog and then click the Next> button.

The command button wizard's second screen is displayed.

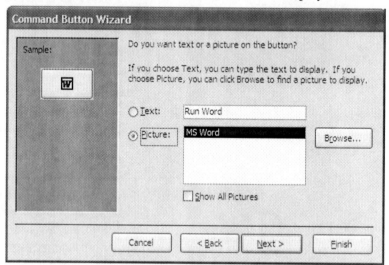

3   Choose the (default) picture icon and click the Next> button.

The command button wizard's final screen is displayed.

Session12

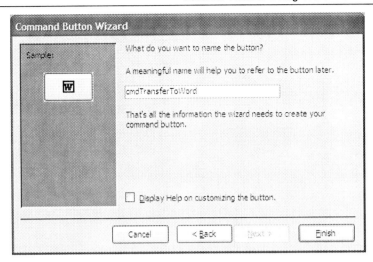

4   Name the button *cmdTransferToWord* and click the *Finish* button.

5   Use Format→Size and Format→Align to make the new button the same vertical height as the *Delete Record* and *Add Record* buttons and Format→Horizontal Spacing→Make equal to perfectly size and position the new button.

The form should now look like this:

6   Switch to Form View and click the cmdTransferToWord button.

The Word application opens but with no document open. In the next lesson we'll refine the click event handler of the new *cmdTransferToWord* command button so that details of the current record are shown using the template designed in the previous lesson.

note

The advantages of Early Binding

The wizard has produced poor quality code by declaring the data type of the *Word Application* object as simply Object. This type of declaration is called *late binding*.

The Object data type is a little like a variant for objects. It is an object variable that does not know what sort of object it relates to.

A higher quality approach would be to declare it as follows:-

```
Dim oWord as _
Word.Application
```

This type of declaration is called *early-binding*.

An early bound object has many advantages: It runs faster as it does not have to be created at runtime and is easier to work with because all of the properties and methods will appear as an IntelliSense pop-up list when you type a dot after the object variable in the code editor.

Early binding also gives you full access to Word's object model via the Object Browser/Help system and the ability to use Word constants (such as *wdGoToBookmark*) within your code.

There is sometimes an argument for using Late Binding when you must support an environment where different versions of Office are in use. For example, the *Word 11 Object library* referenced in the example is a part of Word 2003 so the code will not work on a machine with only Word97 installed unless the reference is changed to *Word 8.0 Object Library*.

Session12a

Lesson 12-3: Transfer data from Access to Word

1   Inspect the code within the cmdTransferToWord button's click event.

```
Private Sub cmdTransferToWord__Click()
On Error GoTo Err_cmdTransferToWord__Click

    Dim oApp As Object

    Set oApp = CreateObject("Word.Application")
    oApp.Visible = True

Exit_cmdTransferToWord__Click:
Exit Sub

Err_cmdTransferToWord__Click:
    MsgBox Err.Description
    Resume cmdTransferToWord__Click
End Sub
```

2   Create a reference to the Word object library.

Choose Tools→References from the VBA code editor window and check the box next to *Word 11.0 Object Library*.

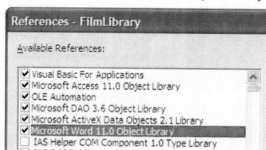

3   Clean up the wizard's code.

As usual the wizard has not written the most elegant code in the world. Improve and simplify the code so that it reads as follows :

```
Private Sub cmdTransferToWord_Click()

On Error GoTo Err_cmdTransferToWord_Click

    Dim oWord As New Word.Application

    With oWord
        .Visible = True
    End With

Exit_cmdTransferToWord__Click:
Exit Sub

Err_cmdTransferToWord__Click:
    MsgBox Err.Description
    Resume cmdTransferToWord__Click
End Sub
```

4   Set the relevant properties, and call the relevant methods of the word object to make the command button work properly.

The With…End With construct makes it simple to work with the Word Application object. Modify the code so that it reads as follows.

```
Private Sub cmdTransferToWord_Click()

On Error GoTo Err_cmdTransferToWord_Click

Dim oWord As New Word.Application

With oWord
    .Documents.Add "Film Details.dot"
    .Selection.GoTo wdGoToBookmark, , , "bmkFilmTitle"
    .Selection.TypeText Me.FilmTitle & " (" & _
    Me.FilmYearReleased & ")"
    .Selection.GoTo wdGoToBookmark, , , "bmkDirector"
    .Selection.TypeText Me.DirectorFullName
    .Selection.GoTo wdGoToBookmark, , , "bmkStudio"
    .Selection.TypeText Me.Studio
    .Selection.GoTo wdGoToBookmark, , , "bmkRating"
    .Selection.TypeText Me.Rating
    .Selection.GoTo wdGoToBookmark, , , "bmkLength"
    .Selection.TypeText Me.FilmLengthMinutes
    .Selection.GoTo wdGoToBookmark, , , "bmkMedia"
    .Selection.TypeText Me.Media
    .Selection.GoTo wdGoToBookmark,,, "bmkPlotOutline"
    .Selection.TypeText Me.FilmPlotOutline
    .Selection.GoTo wdGoToBookmark, , , "bmkReview"
    .Selection.TypeText Me.FilmReview
    .Visible = True
End With

Exit_cmdTransferToWord__Click:
Exit Sub

Err_cmdTransferToWord__Click:
    MsgBox Err.Description
    Resume cmdTransferToWord__Click
End Sub
```

Discussion of how the code works

The code begins by calling the *Add* method of the Word object with the name of the template as a parameter. This causes Word to open a new document based upon the template created earlier. Each of the following line pairs begin by using the *GoTo* method to place the insertion point at the relevant bookmark before using the *TypeText* method to add the correct text to each bookmark.

Film Details
Gone With The Wind (1939)

Director: Fleming, Victor
Studio: Metro-Glodwin-Mayer (MGM)
Rating: U
Length: 233
Media: DVD

Plot Outline: The story of a love affair set in the American deep south during the Civil War.

Review: This film set a new standard for Hollywood blockbusters and box-office numbers of tickets sold have never since been equaled. A new standard was set for colour, sound and cinematography which were pushed to the very limits of the technology of 1939.

Session 12: Exercise

1   Create the following document in Word.

> Dear ¶
> ¶
> I·am·writing·to·confirm·receipt·of·your·order·for··tickets·to·our·special·Wine·Tasting·
> Dinner·at··on·.¶
> ¶
> We·look·forward·to·seeing·you·on·the·night.¶
> ¶
> Best·Regards¶
> ¶
> Laura·Lynn-Hardy··(organiser)¶

2   Add four bookmarks to the document: *bmkName*, *bmkNumberOfTickets*, *bmkDate* and *bmkVenue*. Their position within the text should be obvious.

3   Save the Word document as a document template called *Order Confirmation.dot.*

4   Create a new Access database called *Exercise12.mdb* with a single table called *Order*.

5   Add fields to the table for OrderID, OrderName, OrderNumberOfTickets, OrderDate and OrderVenue.

6   Use the Form Wizard to create a form from the table and save it as frmOrder.

7   Add some sample data to the form.

8   Add a command button to the form called *cmdWordOrderConfirmation* that will start Word with the *Order Confirmation.dot* template and populate the bookmarks with the relevant fields from the form. (Don't forget to add a reference to the *Word Object Library* if required).

9   Test the application.

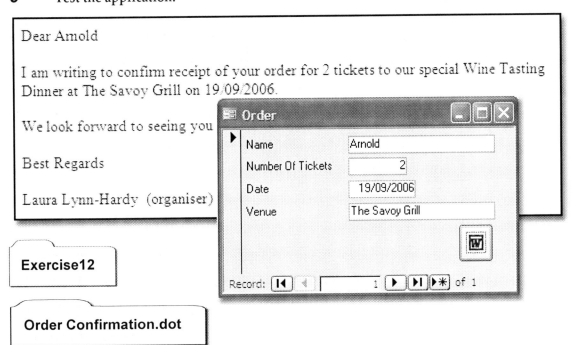

Session 12: Exercise answers

Q4   The table should have been constructed as follows :

	Field Name	Data Type
🔑	OrderID	AutoNumber
	OrderName	Text
	OrderNumberOfTickets	Number
	OrderDate	Date/Time
	OrderVenue	Text

Q8   The code for the *cmdWordOrderConfirmation* command button's *Click* event handler should be similar to the following:

```
Private Sub cmdWordOrderConfirmation_Click()

On Error GoTo Err_cmdWordOrderConfirmation_Click

Dim oWord As New Word.Application

    With oWord
        .Documents.Add "Order Confirmation.dot"
        .Selection.Goto wdGoToBookmark, , , "bmkName"
        .Selection.TypeText Me.OrderName
        .Selection.Goto wdGoToBookmark, , , "bmkNumberOfTickets"
        .Selection.TypeText Me.OrderNumberOfTickets
        .Selection.Goto wdGoToBookmark, , , "bmkDate"
        .Selection.TypeText Me.OrderDate
        .Selection.Goto wdGoToBookmark, , , "bmkVenue"
        .Selection.TypeText Me.OrderVenue

        .Visible = True
    End With

Exit_cmdTransferToWord__Click:
    Exit Sub
Err_cmdTransferToWord__Click:
    MsgBox Err.Description
    Resume cmdTransferToWord__Click
End Sub
```

Session Thirteen: Adding Switchboards, Menus and Toolbars

> Programming today is a race between software engineers striving to build bigger and better idiot-proof programs, and the Universe trying to produce bigger and better idiots. So far, the Universe is winning.
>
> *Rick Cook, The Wizardry Compiled*

At the very beginning of this book we used the Switchboard Wizard to create a switchboard form automatically.

Most professional developers would not use the Switchboard Wizard because manually creating a similar form gives total flexibility over how the form looks and functions.

In this session we're going to create an attractive and functional front-end for the application using a bespoke Switchboard form.

While switchboards are fine if you need to get an application up and running as quickly as possible your users might think them a little old-fashioned and clunky.

Today's computer users are used to sophisticated applications such as the Microsoft Office suite and expect applications to have the same familiar system of drop-down menus and toolbars.

In this session you're going to begin by manually creating a Switchboard form. You'll then provide a better replacement for the Switchboard approach by defining your own custom menus and toolbars to create a truly professionally user interface that (after a little further polishing) will feel greatly superior to a traditional Access application.

Session Objectives

By the end of this session you will be able to:

- Manually create a switchboard form
- Create a global custom menu
- Create a custom toolbar
- Associate menus and toolbars with specific actions

Session13

Lesson 13-1: Create the user interface

note

Finding image files (clipart)

Graphics bring alive applications and make them appear more professional.

There's a wealth of sources for clipart on the Web as well as the clipart collections bundled with other Office applications such as Word and PowerPoint.

A search on the web for the word: *ClipArt* produced over 56 million results so there is plenty to choose from! Make sure that your image is royalty-free (or purchase a licence to use it) if you intend to distribute it as part of a commercial application.

When you find a suitable image simply right-click it in your web browser and choose *Save Picture As…* from the shortcut menu.

Google Images is another great web resource for clipart. A search for *"Film Icon"* produced many images that would be perfect for the Switchboard form.

1. Select the Forms object in the Database window.

2. Double-click *Create form in Design View*.

3. Convert the form to a non-modal dialog by setting the following properties:

Property	Value
Scroll Bars	Neither
Record Selectors	No
Navigation Buttons	No
Dividing Lines	No
Auto Center	Yes
Border Style	Dialog
Min Max Buttons	None
Caption	Switchboard

Note that this time we do not set the *PopUp* and *Modal* properties. That's because we don't want the switchboard to be "always in front" (the *PopUp* property) and want the switchboard to remain in the background while we are doing other things (the *Modal* property).

4. Save the form with the name frmSwitchboard

5. Find a graphic image that conveys the concept of films (see sidebar) and save it to your hard drive.

6. Add an image control to frmSwitchboard.

   The Insert Picture dialog appears.

7. Insert the graphic into the Image control.

8. Re-size the graphic and form so that the graphic fills the left-hand side of the switchboard.

   Your form should now be similar to this:

Session13

9   Add a label control to frmSwitchboard with the following
     properties:

Property	Value
Caption	Film Library Application
Fore Color	8388608
Font Name	Tahoma
Font Size	18
Font Weight	Bold

10   Add a command button to frmSwitchboard.

     The first dialog of the Command Button Wizard appears.

11   Choose Category:*Form operations* and Action:*Open Form*
     and then click the *Next* button.

12   Tell the Wizard that you want to open the frmFilm form and
     click the *Next* button.

13   Tell the Wizard that you want to *Open the form and show all
     the records* and then click the *Next* button.

14   Choose the default graphic and click the *Next* button.

15   Name the button cmdOpenFilmForm and click the *Finish*
     button.

16   Add a label control next to the button and set the *Caption*
     property to *Add/Edit/View Film Data*.

17   Use the command button wizard to create two more buttons.
     One to open the frmFilmReportCriteria form called
     cmdPrintReport and another to quit the application called
     cmdQuit.

     Your form should now look like this:

18   Test the Switchboard form.

Lesson 13-2: Create a custom global menu

The global menu will appear when the user first starts the application. Let's think which features we can safely let the users have without there being any scope to damage our application or cause errors.

The following is a good choice for a bare-bones menu though there are a few other useful options that you might want to make available to users in your own applications :

File	Edit	Tools	Window	Help
Print	Cut	Spelling	Tile Horizontally	Show the Office Assistant
Exit	Copy	Database Utilities-→Compact and Repair Database	Tile Vertically	
	Paste		Cascade	
	Paste Special…			
	Office Clipboard…			

Now that we've designed our custom menu system it's time to implement it.

1   Right-click anywhere in the blank area to the right of the toolbars at the top of your screen and choose Customize from the short cut menu.

2   Click the Toolbars tab and the New... button (Access calls menus toolbars too)!

3   Name the new menu: *mnuMain*.

Session13a

4   Click the *Properties* button within the Customize dialog and set the *Type* property to *Menu Bar* and then click the Close button.

5   Click the *Commands* tab and choose *New Menu* from the Category list.

6   Drag five *New Menu* items onto the new mnuMain toolbar.

Do this by clicking on the New Menu graphic in the right-hand pane of the dialog and dragging on to the empty mnuMain menu bar that should be visible on your screen.

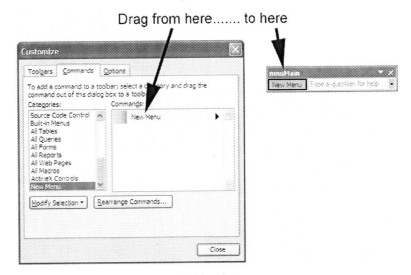

Your toolbar should now look like this:

7   Right-click each of the NewMenu items on the toolbar in turn and change the *Name* property on the shortcut menu to: &File, &Edit, &Tools, &Window and &Help.

Note that the *Name* property on the shortcut menu is confusingly called the *Caption* property if you choose *Properties* from the shortcut menu and re-name your menu items this way.

Your menu bar should now look like this:

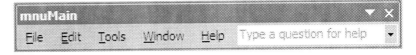

Lesson 13-3: Add standard top-level menus and items

We've now created a set of top-level menus but none of them actually do anything. In this lesson we'll add the drop-down items to each main menu item in order to add the functionality we've decided to allow the user.

1   Right-click anywhere in the blank area to the right of the toolbars at the top of your screen and choose Customize from the short cut menu.

2   Add the required built-in menu items to each of the sub-menus (such as File→Print and File→Exit) by dragging them from the Customize dialog to the *mnuMain* toolbar.

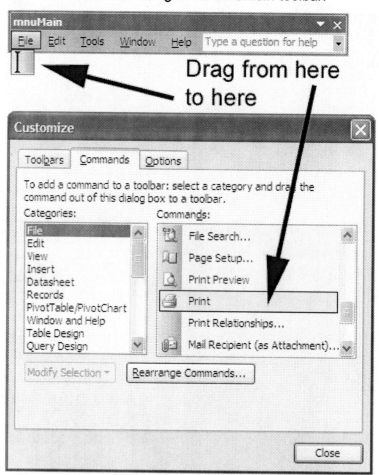

3   Add a dividing line after the File→Print... menu item.

To do this right-click the *Exit* sub-menu item and select *Begin A Group* from the shortcut menu.

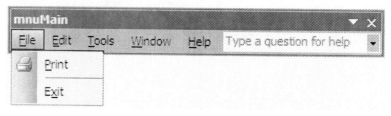

Session13b

4   Use the same technique to create dividing lines for the following groups :

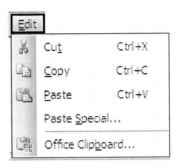

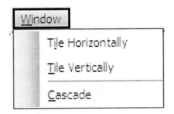

5   Close the Customize dialog box and dock your new menu to the top of the screen.

We now have two menu bars: the standard Access menu bar and your own custom menu bar.

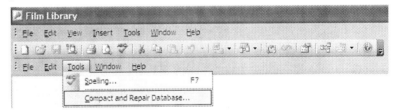

Later we'll learn how to switch off the standard Access menu bar so that the user only sees the replacement *mnuMain* menu bar.

Lesson 13-4: Add a custom top-level menu and items

Next we can think about the actual features of our application and where to put them on the menu system. They are:

■ Show the *frmFilm* form to Add/Edit/Delete film records.

■ Show the *frmReportCriteria* dialog to print out a film report or catalogue.

■ Maintain static data for Directors, Actors, Media Types, Ratings and Studios.

We want to add them to the main menu so that the items appear as regular menu items like this:

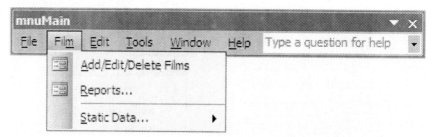

1   Drag a New Menu item onto the mnuMain toolbar so that it is between the *File* and *Edit* main menu items.

Select the *Commands* tab of the *Customize* dialog and then click on the *New Menu* category in the left hand pane. Drag the *New Menu* graphic from the right-hand pane and drop it onto *mnuMain* between the *File* and *Edit* main menu items.

The menu bar should now look like this:

Session13c

2   Right-click the *New Menu* item on *mnuMain* and set the Name property to *Fil&m*.

3   Click *All Forms* in the left hand pane of the Customize dialog and drag the *frmFilm* item to the *mnuMain* menu bar to become the first item in the new *Film* top-level menu.

4   Drag *frmFilmReportCriteria* across to become the second item in the Film menu.

5   Click on the *New Menu* category in the left hand pane of the Customize dialog and drag the *New Menu* item beneath the two items you have just added.

6   Right click each menu item in turn and change the respective Name property to *&Add/Edit/Delete Films*, *&Reports...*, and *&Static Data...*

7   Right click on the *Static Data...* item and choose *Begin a Group* from the shortcut menu to add a dividing line above it and the other menu items.

Your custom menu should now look like this:

8   Click *All Forms* in the left hand pane of the Customize dialog and drag the *frmMaintainDirector* item from the right-hand pane, dropping it slightly to the right of the *Static Data...* item on the *mnuMain* menu bar to become the first item in the new *Static Data...* sub menu.

9   Use the same method to add the *frmMaintain Actor, frmMaintainMedia, frmMaintainRating* and *frmMaintainStudio* forms to the *Static Data...* sub menu.

10   Rename the items you have just added so that the captions (Name properties) are: &Directors, &Actors, &Media, &Ratings and &Studios.

Your menu should now look like this:

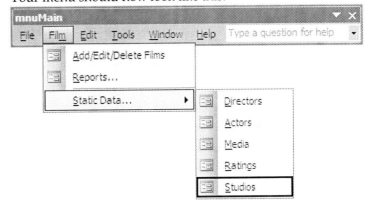

11   Close the *Customize* dialog and test your new menu bar.

Lesson 13-5: Create a custom toolbar

Access allows us to associate a toolbar with a form by simply setting the form's *Toolbar* property to indicate the required toolbar to display.

The *frmFilm* form needs to be able to make use of the fantastically useful *Filter By Form* facility so it makes sense to create a custom toolbar containing the *Filter By Form* icon.

We'll also add a shortcut to display the *frmFilmReportCriteria* dialog from the same toolbar.

1   Right-click anywhere in the blank area to the right of the toolbars at the top of your screen and choose *Customize* from the short cut menu.

   The Customize dialog is displayed.

2   Click the *Toolbars* tab and the *New...* button.

3   Name the new toolbar *tlbFilm* and click the OK button.

4   Click the *Commands* tab, choose the *Records* category then drag the *Filter By Form*, *Filter By Selection* and *Toggle Filter* items onto the new toolbar.

5   Choose the *All Forms* category and drag the *frmFilmReportCriteria* item onto the new toolbar.

6   Right-click on the frmReportCriteria item on the toolbar and change its style to *Text only (Always)* and its Name property to *&Reports...*

   Your custom toolbar should now look like this:

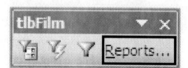

7   Open *frmFilm* in *Design View*. Change the form's *Toolbar* property to *tlbFilm*.

8   Save changes to the form and close it.

9   Switch off any toolbars that are currently on display.

   Do this by right-clicking anywhere in the blank area at the top right of your screen. Uncheck any check-boxes that are checked.

10   Test the form.

   Close and re-open the application – note that no toolbar is displayed though you will see both menus, the standard menu and

Session13d

your own *mnuMain* custom menu.

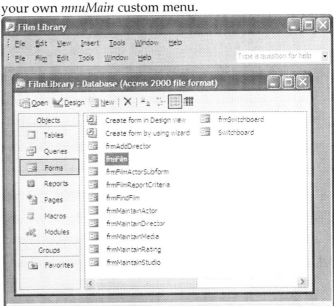

11   Open frmFilm.

Note that your new custom toolbar is displayed only while *frmFilm* is open.

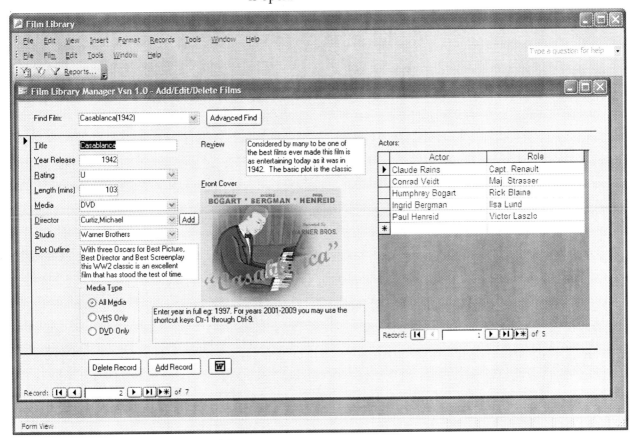

12   Close frmFilm.

Note that the custom toolbar disappears.

Session 13: Exercise

1   Make a copy of your FilmLibrary.mdb file and re-name it *Exercise13.mdb* (there is also an *Exercise13Start.mdb* file available for download from our web site).

2   Enable the *tlbFilm* toolbar so that it is displayed on screen.

3   Add a button to the tlbFilm toolbar that will open the frmFilm form.

4   Give the new button the name *Add/Edit/Delete Films*.

5   Add another button to the tlbFilm toolbar that will display the *Microsoft Office Access Help* icon  when clicked.

Your toolbar should now look like this:

6   Add a new menu item to the *mnuMain* custom menu bar to the right of <u>E</u>dit called <u>V</u>iew.

Your menu bar should now look like this:

7   Add the *Print Preview* and *Zoom* standard Access commands to the View main menu item as sub-menu items.

Your menu bar should now look like this:

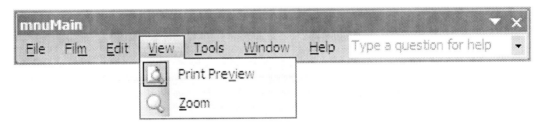

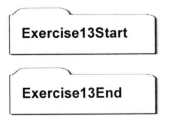

Exercise13Start

Exercise13End

Session 13: Exercise Answers

Q2 Right-click in the blank area, to the right of the toolbars, at the top right of the screen and check the *tlbFilm* item on the shortcut menu.

Q3 Right-click in the blank area, to the right of the toolbars, at the top right of the screen and select *Customize* from the shortcut menu.

Choose the *Commands* tab in the Customize dialog and then the *All Forms* category in the left-hand pane. Drag the command: *frmFilm* from the right-hand pane and drop it onto the toolbar.

Q4 Right-click on the new toolbar button and change the *Name* property to: *&Add/Edit/Delete Films*

Q5 Select the category: *Window and Help* and drag the command *Microsoft Office Access Help* onto the toolbar.

Q6 Select the category: *New Menu* and drag the command: *New Menu* onto the menu bar between the existing *Edit* and *Tools* items.

Right-click on the *New Menu* item on the menu bar and change its *Name* property to *&View*.

Q7 Select the category: *View* and drag the *Print Preview* and *Zoom* commands onto the menu bar as *View* menu sub-menu items.

Session Fourteen: Finalizing The Application For Deployment

> If it looks right it is right.
>
> *Proverb, unknown author*

It's finally time to ready the application for deployment.

The *User Version* of the application will not allow the user access to any of the VBA code we have written or to any Access features that might allow corruption or alteration of any of our Tables, Forms, Reports and other application elements.

Session Objectives

By the end of this session you will be able to:

- QA an application prior to deployment
- Create a user and development version of an application
- Set the application's start-up options

Session14

Lesson 14-1: Implement universal error handling

Before deploying an application you should carefully QA (Quality Assure) all of the VBA code.

All code written should be compliant with your coding standards. Your code should be audited by reference to *The Rules* listed in *Appendix A*.

When you are a more experienced developer you may decide to change or expand some of these rules. It is absolutely vital that you do have a set of written rules, otherwise you will have no standard to audit your own code, and perhaps the code of other programmers if working in a team environment.

You may find that it is convenient to leave certain tasks, such as implementing error handling, closing recordsets, explicitly destroying objects and re-enabling SetWarnings until the QA stage.

Error Handling

We've written many routines without error handling so will implement universal error handling in this lesson.

> **note**
>
> There's nothing more unprofessional (from a client's perspective) than an application that frequently crashes.
>
> One of our most important quality standards *(stated in Appendix A – The Rules)* states that:
>
> *"Error Handling must be implemented in every sub and function without exception".*
>
> Programmers often argue that some code is so simple that it can never fail so does not need error handling. While this may be true in some cases there's nothing wrong with a catch-all approach. If absolutely every sub has error handling code you cannot possibly confront your user with a confidence-sapping runtime error.
>
> When you take this approach it is comforting to find that those bullet-proof subs that couldn't possible fail often do, but when they do the error is always elegantly handled.

1   Open the code editor and add standard error trapping code to every subroutine (without exception).

Here's an example of generic general-purpose error handling code that has been cut and pasted into a simple subroutine. We've deliberately used a sub that could be expected to never fail for the example but still trap the "impossible" error condition!

Before:

```
Private Sub txtFilmYearReleased_Exit(Cancel As Integer)

Me.lblHelp.Caption = ""

End Sub
```

After:

```
Private Sub txtFilmYearReleased_Exit(Cancel As Integer)

On Error GoTo ErrorHandler

Me.lblHelp.Caption = ""

CleanUpAndExit:
Exit Sub

ErrorHandler:
Call MsgBox("An error was encountered" & vbCrLf & _
    vbCrLf & _
    "Description: " & Err.Description & vbCrLf & _
    "Error Number: " & Err.Number, , "Error")
    Resume CleanUpAndExit
End Sub
```

> **Session14**

2   Search your code for all instances of SetWarnings.

Open the code editor and select Edit→Find from the main menu.

Search for the word *SetWarnings* in the entire Current Project.

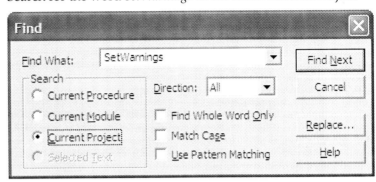

3   Add a single DoCmd.SetWarnings(True) after the CleanUpAndExit: label for any subs that contain this method call.

Whenever you use the SetWarnings(False) method of the DoCmd object you expose your application to a major bug.

If code branches to the Error Handler after the DoCmd.SetWarnings(False) method call but before you re-enable standard Access warnings with a SetWarnings(True) method call there will be no more standard warnings during the entire Access session. This could be potentially disasterous.

Because we have observed the single-exit rule we can simply add a *Call DoCmd.SetWarnings(True)* after the *CleanUpAndExit:* label in order to ensure that warnings are always re-enabled before exiting each affected sub.

```
CleanUpAndExit:

Call DeCmd.SetWarnings(True)
Exit Sub

ErrorHandler:
Call MsgBox("An error was encountered" & vbCrLf & _
    vbCrLf & _
    "Description: " & Err.Description & vbCrLf & _
    "Error Number: " & Err.Number, , "Error")
    Resume CleanUpAndExit
End Sub
```

note

Early and late binding

The wizard has produced poor quality code by declaring the recordset data type as simply *Object*. This type of declaration is called *late binding*.

The Object data type is a little like a variant for objects. It is an object variable that does not know what sort of object it relates to.

A higher quality approach would be to declare it as follows:-

```
Dim rs as DAO.Recordset
```

This type of declaration is called *early-binding*.

An early bound object will run faster as it does not have to be

note

The sample code shows the combo box as being named Combo21. It is quite likely that your code will show it with a different name such as Combo23.

The difference is caused by the Wizard naming controls with an arbitrary number since the control name's only requirement is to be unique.

It would be better to rename the control correctly as *cboFindFilm* but to change both the name of the control and code references to it isn't really worth the effort.

Lesson 14-2: Explicitly declare and destroy objects

Closing recordsets, and explicitly destroying objects

While the need to de-reference object variables is a hotly disputed topic amongst amateur programmers most professionals will always explicitly close recordsets and explicitly de-reference object variables (see sidebar on next page).

Early and late bound objects.

The Access wizards often create late-bound objects (see sidebar).

It is usually a good idea to convert any late-bound objects to explicitly typed early-bound objects. As well as making your application more robust, this type of object will also make your applications run faster.

1   Open the code for the *AfterUpdate* event of the Find Film: combo box on the *frmFilm* form.

```
Private Sub Combo21_AfterUpdate()
On Error GoTo ErrorHandler
    ' Find the record that matches the control.
    Dim rs As Object
    Set rs = Me.Recordset.Clone
    rs.FindFirst "[FilmID] = " & _
    Str(Nz(Me![Combo21].Value, 0))
    If Not rs.EOF Then Me.Bookmark = rs.Bookmark
CleanUpAndExit:
    Exit Sub
ErrorHandler:
Call MsgBox("An error was encountered" & vbCrLf & _
    vbCrLf & _
    "Description: " & Err.Description & vbCrLf & _
    "Error Number: " & Err.Number, , "Error")
    Resume CleanUpAndExit
End Sub
```

This code was originally generated by the combo box wizard and creates a late-bound recordset object called *rs*. There are three problems. The object is early bound, the recordset is not closed, and the object variable is not de-referenced when the sub ends.

2   Add code to early-bind the object.

Change the line:

```
Dim rs As Object
```
to:
```
Dim rs As DAO.recordset
```

3   Add code to explicitly close the recordset.

Add the following code just before *Exit Sub*.

```
rs.Close
```

Session14a

Automatic destruction of object variables

Some programmers argue that Access can automatically de-reference object variables when they go out of scope (in the same way that other types of variables do). It is also sometimes argued that there is no need to explicitly close recordset objects.

It is widely believed that memory leaks (a situation where a computer gradually grinds to a halt as the memory becomes exhausted and then needs to be re-booted) are often caused by relying upon automatic destruction. For this reason most professional programmers always close record sets and explicitly de-reference object variables.

It is instructive to examine the wizard-generated Switchboard form's HandleButtonClick function. You will find that Microsoft also find value in

Subs and functions that require attention

frmAddDirector:
cmdOK_Click()

frmFilm:
cmdTransferToWord_Click()

frmFindFilm:
cmdShowSelectedFilm_Click()

Note that while the Switchboard form has non-compliant code it no longer forms part of the application so does not have to be Quality Assured.

It has been left in the application only because the wizard-generated code is interesting to study.

4   Add code to explicitly destroy (de-reference) the object.

Add the following code on the next line:

```
Set rs = Nothing
```

This will explicitly de-reference the object variable and cause it to be destroyed. The last section of the code should now look like this:

```
    If Not rs.EOF Then Me.Bookmark = rs.Bookmark
    rs.Close ' Close the recordset
    Set rs = Nothing ' Destroy the object
    Exit Sub
ErrorHandler:

Call MsgBox("An error was encountered" & vbCrLf & _
    vbCrLf & _
    "Description: " & Err.Description & vbCrLf & _
    "Error Number: " & Err.Number, , "Error")
End Sub
```

5   Improve code to clean up after error conditions.

We also have to guard against the possibility of the error handler being invoked before the recordset is opened or instantiated. This could cause a severe error condition called a *recursive loop* when the code will run around in circles and hang the application.

To solve the problem we use the *On Error Resume Next* statement to bypass error handling if there is no recordset to close or no instantiated object to destroy.

The last section of the code should now look like this:

```
    If Not rs.EOF Then Me.Bookmark = rs.Bookmark

CleanUpAndExit:
    ' Close the recordset defensively
    On Error Resume Next
    rs.Close
    ' Destroy the object defensively
    On Error Resume Next
    Set rs = Nothing
Exit Sub

ErrorHandler:
Call MsgBox("An error was encountered" & vbCrLf & _
    vbCrLf & _
    "Description: " & Err.Description & vbCrLf & _
    "Error Number: " & Err.Number, , "Error")
    Resume CleanUpAndExit
End Sub
```

6   Improve code in the other three subs that instantiate object variables (see sidebar for listing).

Lesson 14-3: Improve form appearance

All forms have a similar appearance and include standard Access features such as Record Selectors, Navigator Bars and Dividing Lines.

While there's nothing at all wrong with retaining these features we can give the application a more crisp, modern feel by eliminating items that add no value to the form.

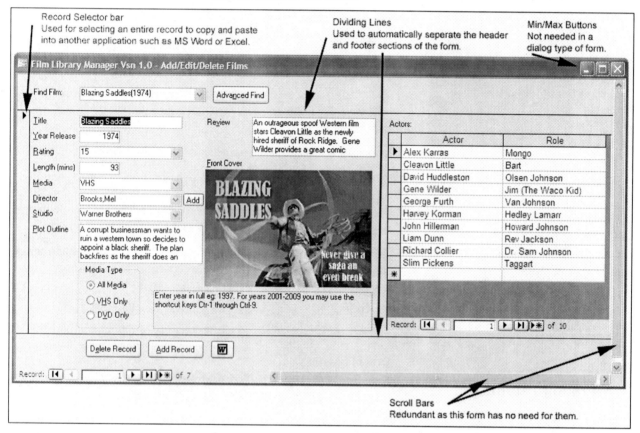

Record Selector bar
Used for selecting an entire record to copy and paste
into another application such as MS Word or Excel.

Dividing Lines
Used to automatically seperate the header
and footer sections of the form.

Min/Max Buttons
Not needed in a
dialog type of form.

Scroll Bars
Redundant as this form has no need for them.

1 **Eliminate redundant items from all forms.**

Set the following form properties for *frmFilm* as well as the static data maintenance forms *frmMaintainActor*, *frmMaintainDirector*, *frmMaintainMedia*, *frmMaintainRating* and *frmMaintainStudio*.

Property	Value
Scroll Bars	Neither
Record Selectors	No
Dividing Lines	No
Auto Center	Yes
Border Style	Dialog
Min Max Buttons	None

tip

If you hold down the <Shift> key before selecting the *Line* control you will be able to draw perfectly horizontal lines.

2   Add two horizontal lines to de-lineate the top and bottom sections of the frmFilm form.

Now that we've removed the Access-specific dividing lines we can draw two horizontal lines onto the face of the form but this time we have total control over where they will be.

Use the Line control ╲ from the Control Toolbox to draw the lines.

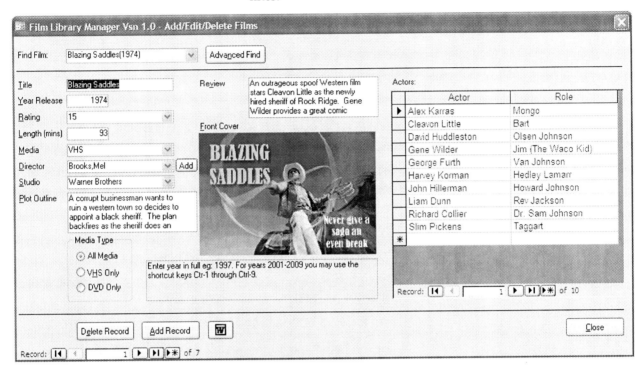

Lesson 14-4: Further improve form appearance

The navigator bar is a common feature of Access forms and automatically provides a means to navigate the recordset and add new records.

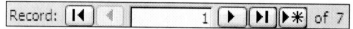

The navigator bar attached to the *Actors* subform (on the *frmFilm* form) is entirely redundant since we can navigate actor records, add new actor records, and delete the relationship between actor records and film records without using the navigator bar.

Unlike the subform navigation bar, the main navigator bar on *frmFilm* is probably worth keeping as it provides an easy way to navigate records and also informs of the number of records in the recordset and whether a filter condition is active.

If you really don't like the appearance of the navigation bar it is possible to replace it with custom command buttons (the command button wizard can automatically generate robust code to do this).

1   Open frmFilmActorSubform in Design View.

2   Set the *Navigation Buttons* property to *No*.

3   Close the subform and open frmFilm. Note that the *Actors* subform no longer has navigation buttons.

4   Add a Close button to the bottom-right of the frmFilm form.

   Use the Command Button wizard to add a close button to the bottom right hand corner of the form. Name the command button *cmdClose* and give it a caption of *&Close*.

   Set the Close button's *Cancel* property to *Yes* so that the user can also close the form using the <Escape> key.

   Use Format→Size and Format→Align from the main menu to make the button exactly the same size as the *Add Record* and *Delete Record* buttons, top-aligned with the other buttons and right-aligned with the *Actors* sub-form.

   Your frmFilm form should now look like this:

Session14c

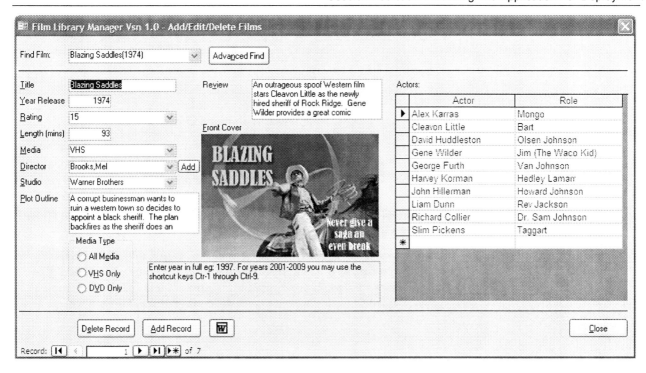

Lesson 14-5: Setting startup options

note

never say never!

"Never say never, for if you live long enough, chances are you will not be able to abide by its restrictions. Never is a long, undependable time, and life is too full of rich possibilities to have restrictions placed upon it".

Gloria Swanson,
US actress (1899 - 1983)

A statement such as "There really is no way to open the application once it is locked" would be regarded by hackers as a challenge.

At time of writing I do not know of any way to regain access to an Access database that has been locked in the way described in this lesson. It is, however, quite possible that a hacker will discover a way of doing this in the future.

We are now ready to lock the application down so that even the most determined user can't make any changes to it.

If there were some sort of "backdoor" or other trickery that would allow you to break into the application once it is secured this would defeat the object of locking it. It is thus vitally important that you save two versions of your application before you lock down the user version or you will have locked your work and thrown away the key! There really is no way to open the application once it is locked.

1   Close Access and then make two copies of your application. Re-name one *FilmLibrary Version 1 Development* and the other *FilmLibrary Version 1 User*.

2   Open *FilmLibrary Version 1 User*.

3   From the main menu select Tools→Startup…

The Startup dialog is displayed.

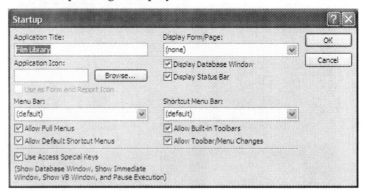

4   Set the following Startup options.

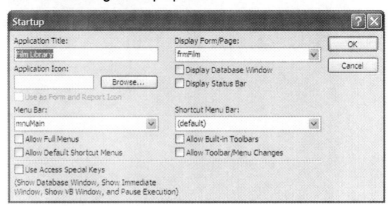

Session14d

Option	Set to	What it does
Application Title	Film Library	Sets the text that will be displayed on the top status bar while the application is running.
Application Icon	None set	Changes the icon that will show in the title bar of the application and on the bottom toolbar when minimized.
Use as Form and Report Icon	unchecked	Will show the same icon on the top left of all forms and reports.
Menu Bar	mnuMain	Will replace the standard Access menu with our more restricted custom menu to prevent the user from damaging the application.
Allow full menus	unchecked	Prevents the user from getting access to potentially damaging Access functionality that does not exist in our custom menu.
Allow default shortcut menus	unchecked	Disables all Access shortcut menus to guard against the possibility of potentially damaging functionality being exposed.\n\nSetting this parameter means that you must provide the user with a button for deleting records on forms as you have already disabled the other three methods (toolbar, main menu, and selecting and pressing the <delete> key) of doing this.\n\nBecause we have already provided a Delete button on all forms it is safe to uncheck this option.
Display Form/ Page	frmFilm	Will display the frmFilm dialog as the default form when the application is opened.
Display Database Window	unchecked	Prevents the user from accessing, deleting or changing forms, reports, queries and other objects from the database window.
Display status bar	unchecked	Disables the Access-specific bottom status bar.
Allow built-in toolbars	unchecked	Prevents the user from accessing potentially damaging Access features by enabling toolbars.
Allow toolbar/menu changes	unchecked	Prevents the user from accessing potentially damaging Access features by customising toolbars to add features.
Use special access keys	unchecked	Prevents the user (and the developer) from undoing any of the above restrictions (use with caution).

5   Close the application and re-open it.

All of the startup options come into force. It is now impossible to damage the application when using the *User Version* of the application.

Lesson 14-6: Test the application

Before an application is released to users it should be thoroughly tested to ensure that there are no bugs or rough edges to it.

1   Open FilmLibrary Version 1 User.

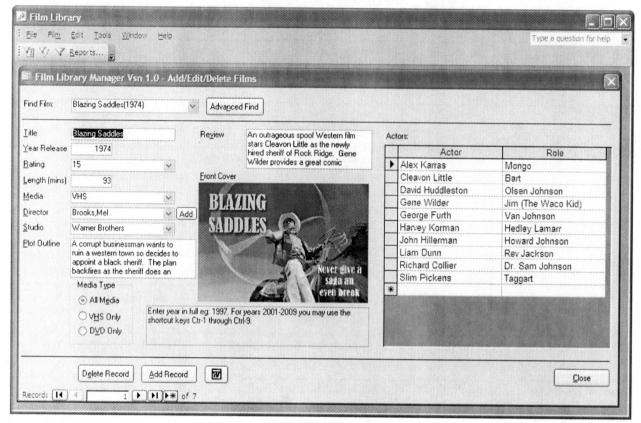

The main form is displayed. Note the custom menu bar and the custom toolbar for this form.

2   Test the form

Try to complete every operation a user might try and also some that a user probably wouldn't.

Whatever you do it should be impossible to create an unhandled error or problem.

3   Click the Advanced Find button.

The advanced find dialog is displayed.

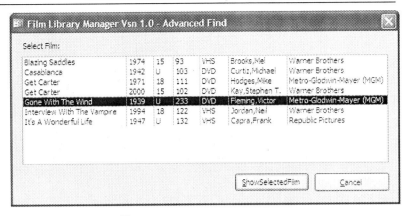

4   Double-click any film.

The film is displayed on the screen.

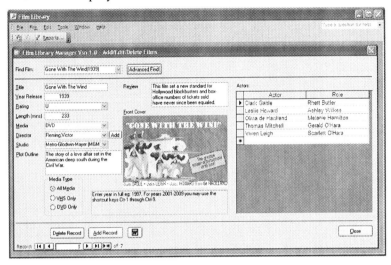

5   Click the Reports... button on the top toolbar.

The *Report Criteria* dialog is displayed.

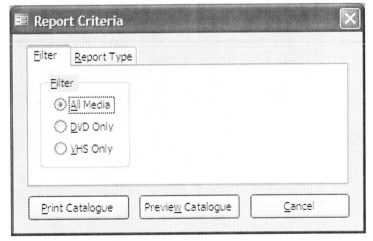

6   Click the *Preview Catalogue* button.

The film catalogue report is shown in *Print Preview* view.

7   Close the report and select File→Exit from the main menu.

The application ends.

Session 14: Exercise

1   The following code works fine but it needs some attention to meet quality standards (as documented in *Appendix A – The Rules*). See if you can identify the corrections needed.

```
Private Sub cmdOK_Click()

Dim rs As DAO.Recordset

Set rs = Forms!frmFilm.cboDirector.Recordset

Call rs.FindFirst("Director = '" & Me.txtDirectorLastName & _
"," & Me.txtDirectorFirstName & "'")
If rs.NoMatch = False Then
    Call MsgBox("This director has already been added")
Else
    Me.Refresh
    Forms!frmFilm.cboDirector.Requery
    Forms!frmFilm.cboDirector.SetFocus
    Forms!frmFilm.cboDirector.Text = Me.txtDirectorLastName & "," & _
    Me.txtDirectorFirstName
    DoCmd.Close
End If

End Sub
```

Session 14: Exercise answers

No error handling has been implemented. This should be done by adding standard error-handling code as follows:

```
Private Sub cmdOK_Click()
On Error GoTo ErrorHandler
    Existing Code
CleanUpAndExit:
Exit Sub
ErrorHandler:
Call MsgBox("An error was encountered" & vbCrLf & _
    vbCrLf & _
    "Description: " & Err.Description & vbCrLf & _
    "Error Number: " & Err.Number, , "Error")
    Resume CleanUpAndExit
End Sub
```

A recordset object has been opened and not closed.

This can be corrected by adding the code:

```
On Error Resume Next
rs.Close
```

Just after the CleanUpAndExit: label.

An object variable has been instantiated but not de-referenced

This can be corrected by adding the code:

```
On Error Resume Next
Set rs = Nothing
```

Just after the rs.Close method call.

The Error handling code should now read:

```
    Existing Code
CleanUpAndExit:

On Error Resume Next
rs.Close
On Error Resume Next
Set rs = Nothing
Exit Sub

ErrorHandler:
Call MsgBox("An error was encountered" & vbCrLf & _
    vbCrLf & _
    "Description: " & Err.Description & vbCrLf & _
    "Error Number: " & Err.Number, , "Error")
    Resume CleanUpAndExit
End Sub
```

Appendix A: The Rules

Rules are for the obedience of fools and the guidance of wise men.

Douglas Bader (British World War II fighter pilot) 1910-1982

The very best programmers are those that are fanatical about rules.

Some rules are so self-evidently good and great that it's almost impossible to find a programmer that could disagree with them. For example The *Cradle to the Grave naming convention* is a very simple rule that saves a massive amount of time and cost when programming any project and makes information systems a delight to work with.

Proposing some rules can cause debate, and even sometimes anger, amongst programmers who do not want to change the way they are used to programming. For this reason, whenever a team project is undertaken it is a good ideal to publish the rules and spend the first morning in a meeting to ensure that all programmers agree and "buy into" them. During this meeting it must be made clear that all rules are entirely negotiable providing that a case for changes can be logically argued. Some of our best rules have come from these brainstorming sessions.

The rules presented in this Appendix are a subset of The Smart Method's own rules that include generally accepted best-practice as well as some of our own unique standards. Rules that apply to advanced concepts not introduced in this book (such as user defined objects) are not included in order to avoid confusion.

We use the "rule book" to QA all code prior to releasing the first version of an application to a client. All code in this book should conform to the rules (mistakes excepted).

You don't need to adopt The Smart Method's rules but they are a good starting point to derive your own rules.

Never be afraid to break the rules when you have good reason to. As Douglas Bader observed, they are only for guidance. When you do break the rules, however, make sure you can justify (to yourself at least) why you did it!

Never break the rules in a misguided attempt to save time by producing "quick and dirty" code. You'll waste far more time unravelling the mess than you'll ever save (but programmers still do this over and over again)!

Visual Basic is all-powerful and with power comes responsibility. Use the power wisely, adhere to this programming standard (or your own derivative of it) and write beautiful, robust code.

1: General rules

1-1   Apart from prefixes and spaces exactly the same name is used for the field name, caption (for the form control that maintains the data), report column header and code variable name. We call this the "Cradle to the Grave Naming Convention".

> We can trace the footsteps of St. Patrick almost from his cradle to his grave by the names of places called after him.
>
> *E. Cobham Brewer 1810–1897. Dictionary of Phrase and Fable.*

Good:

Field name:	CustomerFirstName	(table name prefix)
Field caption:	First Name	(space added for clarity)
Report column header:	First Name	
Form caption:	First Name	
Code variable:	strFirstName	(data type prefix, no spaces)

Bad:

Field name:	CustFName
Field caption:	Christian Name
Report column header:	Given Name
Form caption:	Name
Code variable:	strFNm

Believe it or not the second example is, almost universally, what you will find in the real world of commercial applications. Badly informed managers often erroneously believe that hacking together low-quality applications will result in them being completed faster. A very important responsibility of your job as a development professional is to educate and inform so that this doesn't happen!

1-2   There must only be one exit in any sub or function.

Code that has multiple exits is confusing to read and causes problems with cleanup code (such as closing recordsets, de-referencing objects, destroying objects and ensuring that warnings are always re-enabled).

Good:

```
Function CodeToName( strCategory as string) as string

Dim strReturn as string
IF strCategory = "MAN" Then
    strReturn = "Manchester"
Elseif strCategory = "LHR" Then
    strReturn = "London Heathrow"
Else
    strReturn = "Unknown"
End If
    CodeToName = strReturn
End Function
```
(Error handling code not shown)

Bad:

```
Function CodeToName( strCategory as string) as string

IF strCategory = "MAN" Then
    CodeToName = "Manchester"
```

```
        Exit Function
Elseif strCategory = "LHR" Then
        CodeToName = "London Heathrow"
        Exit Function
Else
        CodeToName = "Unknown"
        Exit Function
End If
End Function
```

Be particularly careful not to violate the single exit rule in error handling code.

Good:

```
Private Sub txtFilmYearReleased_Exit(Cancel As Integer)
        On Error GoTo ErrorHandler
        Me.lblHelp.Caption = ""
CleanUpAndExit:
        Exit Sub
ErrorHandler:
        Call MsgBox("An error was encountered" & vbCrLf & _
            vbCrLf & _
            "Description: " & Err.Description & vbCrLf & _
            "Error Number: " & Err.Number, , "Error")
        Resume CleanUpAndExit
End Sub
```

Bad:

```
Private Sub txtFilmYearReleased_Exit(Cancel As Integer)
        On Error GoTo ErrorHandler
        Me.lblHelp.Caption = ""
        Exit Sub
ErrorHandler:
        Call MsgBox("An error was encountered" & vbCrLf & _
            vbCrLf & _
            "Description: " & Err.Description & vbCrLf & _
            "Error Number: " & Err.Number, , "Error")
End Sub
```

1-3 Use mixed case names, no underscores and capitalised first letter throughout for sub, function, variable, field, object and control names.

Good:

```
strCompanyPostCode
txtCompanyPostCode
GetCompanyPostCode()
```

Bad:

```
strCompany_Post_Code
txtcompanypostcode
GetCompanypostcode()
```

By never using underscores in your own sub and function names it will always be obvious which subs are event handlers.

By never using underscores in variable names it will always be easy to differentiate between variables and constants.

1-4   Name variables in the form Noun or Noun–Verb.

Because of our *Cradle to the Grave Naming Convention* just about every variable name that relates to a field will begin with a noun. This is because every entity (table name) in the system is usually a noun. For example:

```
strCustomerFirstName
strCustomerLastName
strCustomerPostCode
```

Boolean variables often include a verb.

Good: `blnCustomerIsValid, blnCustomerHasCar`

Bad: `blnIsValidCustomer, blnHasCarCustomer`

1-5   Name subs and functions as in the spoken word.

All function and sub names should read just like the spoken English word. This makes code less quirky and nearer to "real life".

Good:

```
AddCustomer
DeleteCustomer
CalculateMovingAverage
GetCustomerByPrimaryKey
```

Bad:

```
CustomerAdd
CustomerDelete
MovingAverageCalculate
CustomerGetByPrimaryKey
```

You should be aware that there is a contrary school of thought (to which we do not subscribe) that suggests that subs and functions should be named in the form of noun-verb. The advantage of this approach is that an alphabetic listing of all sub and function names will group all subs relevant to a specific entity (such as Customer) together.

1-6   Never use abbreviations for table, field—or any other—names.

> A good yardstick for choosing a name is to try to imagine that there is an extraordinary reward for two programmers if they can independently come up with the same program text for the same problem. Both programmers know the reward, but cannot otherwise communicate. Such an experiment would be futile, of course, for any sizable problem, but it is a neat goal. The reward of real life is that a program written by someone else, which is identical to what one's own program would have been, is extremely readable and modifiable.
>
> *Dr. Charles Simonyi (formerly Microsoft's Chief Architect)*

Example: A table contains Customer data. One of the fields in the table contains the Customer's first name.

Good: `strCustomerFirstName`

Bad: `strCustFNm, strCstmFName`

If you were playing Charles Simonyi's game and you needed to guess which name another programmer had come up with for a variable containing information of data type string that contains a Customer's first name you'd probably win (with strCustomerFirstName) in the first example above but would probably lose with the second two.

A long time ago, when visual basic didn't have a compiler and memory was a precious commodity, there was a small performance gain to be had by abbreviating names. There isn't any more (and hasn't been for some years). So why do 21st century programmers still create cryptic, bug prone, and difficult-to-maintain code by abbreviating names? It is one of the great mysteries of life!

Some programmers argue that you don't have to type as much if you use abbreviations. You may save a few keystrokes when you write the code but you'll waste many hours later on when you have to analyse every sub in order to establish what your cryptically named variables actually contain.

1-7   **Name tables, fields—and everything else—in the singular.**

As mentioned in the previous rule, One of the goals of our naming convention is that programmers should be able to intuitively guess the correct name of any variable or function.

The use of plurals makes this goal more difficult. Consider a *GetCompanyType(lngCompanyType)* function that returns zero, one or more company records. Without this rule programmers would have to guess whether the correct function was *GetCompanyType()* or *GetCompanyTypes()*.

This problem is avoided by only ever using singular names for variables, tables, subroutines, directory (folder) names, web page names, file names and field names.

The single exception to this rule is in the naming of object collections. While we haven't covered creating your own object collections in this book you can see that Microsoft adhere to this standard within the Access object model. For example the Forms collection contains many Form objects and the Controls collection contains many Control objects.

About Table Naming

You should be aware that some database designers turn this convention upside down and make all table names plural. It is (vastly) preferable to enforce an "everything in the singular" convention as field names must preficed with the table name (see *table and field naming rules*) and would look very confusing in the plural.

1-8   **Do not use "Magic Numbers".**

Never use numeric values as control variables. Instead, include a globally visible constant.

Good: `GetCompany( TSM_NORTH_WEST_AREA_ONLY )`
Bad: `GetCompany( 23 )`

1-9   **Strongly type all function and sub parameters.**

Good: `Function GetCustomer( lngCustomerID as Long )`
Bad: `Function GetCustomer( lngCustomerID)`

1-10   **Declare all parameters ByVal unless there is a good reason to declare them ByRef.**

Good: `Function GetCustomer( ByVal lngCustomerID as Long )`
Bad: `Function GetCustomer( lngCustomerID)`
         `Function GetCustomer( ByRef lngCustomerID)`

Both of the two "bad" cases above are functionally equivalent because *ByRef* is the default method of passing arguments.

Good reasons to pass parameters ByRef would include code that must be heavily optimised for speed and a low memory footprint or the requirement to return multiple values from a sub or function.

1-11   **Do not use globally scoped variables.**

The use of global variables violates the concept of encapsulation. Global variables also result in buggy code that is difficult to maintain and prevents code re-use as code becomes reliant upon a supporting infrastructure.

Note that this rule does not apply to global constants.

1-12 Do not use the addition operator for concatenating strings.

Use & for concatenating strings and + only for arithmetic operations.

1-13 Avoid *Exit For* and *Exit Do*

> If you use an Exit Do, people will think less of you.
>
> *Button seen at programmer's convention – unknown author.*

Bailing out of loops can cause the same problems as having multiple exits in subs as it makes code less readable and more prone to bugs. Unless there is no reasonable alternative avoid doing this.

1-14 Use the Call statement when calling subs and functions.

Consider the following example:

Without the *Call* statement

```
strCustomerName = GetCustomerName( lngCustomerID)
DeleteCustomer lngCustomerID
MsgBox "You have successfully deleted customer: " & strCustomerName
```

With the *Call* statement

```
strCustomerName = GetCustomerName( lngCustomerID)
Call DeleteCustomer( lngCustomerID)
Call MsgBox( "you have successfully deleted customer: " & strCustomerName )
```

The second example reads more cleanly than the first because the three function calls use identical syntax (brackets de-lineate arguments). For this reason *Call* should be used in every case when calling functions, subs and object methods.

1-15 Never rely upon the default properties of objects.

VBA has a very confusing "feature" in that every control has a default property...

```
txtCustomerFirstName.Value = "John"
```
and
```
txtCustomerFirstName = "John"
```

...are functionally equivalent because *Value* is the default property of a *Text Box* control.

The default property feature has (thankfully) been removed from the latest versions of stand-alone VB (VB.Net and VB 2005) showing that Microsoft also agree that it isn't the best feature in the world.

Never use default properties in your VBA code as they make the code less readable and more prone to error (as the actual property being manipulated must remain in the programmer's memory).

2: Table and Field naming

2-1 Never use prefixes for table names.

Access developers commonly prefix table names with *tbl*. We don't like this convention. The primary object in an Access database is the table so we prefer the *lack of* any prefix to identify this type of object.

Table name prefixes are also incompatible with the "Field names are always prefixed by the table name" rule.

2-2   **Primary keys are named using the syntax: <table name> + <ID>**

Example: Table named *Customer*
Primary Key: *CustomerID*

2-3   **Foreign keys always have exactly the same name as the related primary key.**

Example: The primary key *MediaID* in the *Media* table is also called *MediaID* when used as a foreign key in the *Film* table.

2-4   **If not obvious, the unit of measure is incorporated into the field name.**

Example: A field is needed to indicate the length of a film. It is not clear whether the data will be expressed in hours or minutes.

Good: FilmLengthMinutes
Bad: FilmLength

2-5   **The link table in a many-to-many relationship is always named with the names of the tables on either side of the many-to-many relationship.**

Example: Two tables have a many-to-many relationship, the *Film* and *Actor* tables.

A link table named *FilmActor* is created to model the relationship.

2-6   **Apart from Foreign Keys, field names are always prefixed by the table name.**

This is one of those golden rules that (in conjunction with the *Cradle to the Grave Naming Convention*) will massively increase your productivity and the reliability of your code.

Because all table names in a database are unique, every field name in your database (apart from Primary and Foreign Keys) will also be unique if you prefix all field names with table names. This provides huge benefits:

- Many reporting tools (including Access) have query designers that automatically create joins for fields of the same name. Because we have a rule that foreign and primary keys always have the same name, the query designer will get it right every single time. There will never be any spurious joins caused by occurrences of the same non-key field name in different tables.

- SQL queries become a lot simpler when this rule is in place as you will not have to explicitly qualify every field name with a reference to the related table.

- Code becomes more readable and less error-prone:
  ```
  strCustomerFirstName = "James" ' I know this originated in the Customer Table
  strEmployeeFirstName = "Peter" ' I know this originated in the Employee Table
  strFirstName = "Paul" ' Which table did this come from?  I'll have to guess or
                        ' trace the code.
  ```

Example: All field names in the Film table are prefixed with the word *Film* so have names such as *FilmTitle, FilmYearReleased* and *FilmReview*.

3: Field properties

3-1   **Primary keys are always meaningless and have the data type:** *AutoNumber*.

3-2   **The default value of non-required foreign keys should be Null and not 0 (the Access default).**

Since the data type of primary keys must always be *AutoNumber* it follows that the data type of foreign keys are always numeric. It will not be possible to add records to a child table if it has a foreign key (that forms part of a constrained relationship) with a value of 0.

3-3 At least one (non primary key) field must always be required.

This rule will prevent users from accidentally creating entirely blank records. While observing this rule avoid non-essential required fields, only making them so when business rules demand it.

4: Access object naming

4-1 Prefix objects with the following letters in lower case:

Object	Prefix
Table	No prefix
Query	qry
Form	frm
Report	rpt
Macro	mcr
Module	mod

Example: *frmFilm*.

5: Form control naming

5-1 Use generally accepted three-letter standard prefixes for all form controls. Some of the more common prefixes are:

Prefix	Object Type	Example
cbo	Combo Box and Drop Down List Box	cboEnglish
chk	Checkbox	chkReadOnly
cmd	Command Button	cmdOK
ctr	Control (when specific type is unknown)	ctrCurrent
dat	Data control	datFilm
dir	Directory list box	dirSource
dlg	Common Dialog Control	dlgFileOpen
frm	Form	frmEntry
fra	Frame	fraStyle
img	Image	imgIcon
lbl	Label	lblHelpMessage

lin	Line	linVertical
lst	List Box	lstPolicyCodes
mnu	Menu	mnuFileOpen
opt	Option Button	optRed
ole	OLE Control	oleWorksheet
pic	Picture	picHotel
spn	Spin Control	spnPages
txt	Text Box	txtLastName
tmr	Timer	tmrAlarm

6: Variable naming

6-1   **Module scoped variables must be prefixed with the letter *m* and globally scoped variables must be prefixed with the letter *g*.**

Note that, despite this standard, it is nearly always poor programming practice to use any globally visible variables in an application (note that this rule does not apply to globally visible constants that are extremely useful).

```
mstrCustomerName          ' Module level
strCustomerName           ' Local to sub
gstrApplicationLanguage   ' Globally visible
```

6-2   **Use generally accepted three-letter variable prefixes.**

Microsoft publish recommended three-letter variable prefixes in their MSDN library and these are generally accepted by professional programmers.

Some of the more common prefixes are:

Data Type	Prefix
String	str
Long integer	lng
Boolean	bln
Currency	cur
Double	dbl
Variant	vnt (var also acceptable)
Date and Time	dat (dtm also acceptable)

The alternative prefixes for Variant and Date and Time above are so commonly used that both can be allowed as similies within code.

Early code was often written with one letter variable type prefixes (such as s for string). There's even examples in wizard-generated code of two-letter variable prefixes (such as st for string) but neither style is often seen today.

7: Constants

7-1 Name constants using upper case and underscores.

Programmers should always be aware of which variables are constants. Clearly identify them by always using the upper-case/underscore style for constant names (and only for constant names). It will then always be easy to differentiate between variables and constants in your code.

Good: `TSM_APPLICATION_STATUS`
Bad: `conApplicationStatus`

You'll often see code written using the "bad" convention above. Note that Microsoft do not observe this rule with their own constants such as *vbRed*.

7-2 Constants should always be named with a prefix that is unlikely to be used by any other third party code.

Microsoft use the prefix vb for all of their constants. You should use at least three letters, perhaps your own initials or the name of the application you are writing. As there are 27^3 combinations of three-letter prefixes it is unlikely (though not impossible) that your constant prefixes will coincide with those used by a third party library.

8: Variable declaration

8-1 The *Require Variable Declaration* option must always be switched on.

This can be done by selecting Tools→Options from the code editor window. The *Option Explicit* command will then be included at the top of every new (but not existing) module.

8-2 All variables must be strongly typed.

This includes variables declared as parameters for subs and functions.

Good: `Dim strFirstName as string`
        `Sub DeleteCustomer( lngCustomerID as Long)`
Bad: `Dim strFirstName`
        `Sub DeleteCustomer( lngCustomerID)`

8-3 All variables must be declared and typed with a dedicated Dim statement.

It is possible to declare more than one variable within a single *Dim* statement but this practice can cause problems.

At first glance you may think that:
`Dim strOne,strTwo as string`

Was functionally equivalent to:
`Dim strOne as String`
`Dim strTwo as String`

The first example would, in fact, declare *strOne* as a Variant and only *strTwo* as a string.

Good:
`Dim strFirstName as string`
`Dim strLastName as string`

Bad:
`Dim strFirstName, strLastName as string ' first variable is a variant`

8-4   When declaring variables and constants include an in-line comment detailing their purpose.

Example:
```
dim lngFormMode as long          ' Can be TSM_FORM_INSERT or TSM_FORM_UPDATE
dim lngCompanyCount as long       ' Used to iterate through rsCompanies
dim blnCompanyIsActive as boolean ' Flags current credit status
```

9: Error handling

9-1   Error handling must be implemented in every sub and function *without exception.*

Programmers often argue that some code is so simple that it can never fail so does not need error handling. While this may be true in some cases there's nothing wrong with a catch-all approach. If absolutely every subroutine has error handling you cannot possibly confront your user with an unprofessional and confidence-sapping runtime error. When you take this approach it is comforting to find that those bullet-proof subs that couldn't possible fail often do, but when they do the error is gracefully handled.

9-2   Whenever SetWarnings methods are used in a function or sub a call to SetWarnings(True) must be included immediately before the single exit point (within the clean up code section).

If code branches to the Error Handler after the DoCmd.SetWarnings(False) method call but before you re-enable standard Access warnings with a DoCmd.SetWarnings(True) method call there will be no more standard warnings during the entire Access session. This could be potentially disasterous. Adding a precautionary SetWarnings(True) call within the cleanup section eliminates exposure to this problem.

10: Object destruction

10-1   Recordsets that are opened must be explicitly closed.

10-2   All objects that are instantiated must be explicitly destroyed when no longer needed.

This has been a "hot topic" amongst VBA programmers and fiercely debated on the programming bulletin boards for years.

Some programmers argue that Access can automatically de-reference object variables when they go out of scope (in the same way that other types of variables do).

It is widely believed that memory leaks (a situation where a computer gradually grinds to a halt as the memory becomes exhausted and then needs to be re-booted) are often caused by relying upon automatic object destruction.

It is instructive to examine the wizard-generated code for Access switchboards. The code within the *HandleButtonClick* function shows that Microsoft also find value in closing recordsets and explicitly destroying objects when working with their own product.

Appendix B: Useful Links

> When I took office, only high energy physicists had ever heard of what is called the Worldwide Web.... Now even my cat has its own page.
>
> *Bill Clinton*
> *Announcement of Next Generation Internet initiative, 1996*

Everything you could ever want to know, and a lot of things you wouldn't want to know, are available somewhere upon the magnificent unstructured mess that is the Internet. All that is needed is to know where to look.

I've often hunted for the answer to a simple question on the Internet for hours and still not found it.

Part of the problem is that the integrity of the information presented upon the web is extremely variable. It is difficult to establish whether the information is coming from a seasoned professional or Bill Clinton's cat. The links provided upon the following pages will point you at some of the good guys on the web.

Because the web is ever-changing, however, there's a good chance that some, or even most, of the links will no longer work by the time you read this book. For this reason you'll only really ever need one link:

www.LearnAccessVba.com

We'll keep all of the links described on the following pages up-to-date on this site.

Useful web site links

This book's dedicated web site.

http://www.learnaccessvba.com

All sample code in this book and an updated version of this links list can be found here.

In time we'll develop this site into a really useful place for Access developer's to visit and share tips and tricks.

The Smart Method. Our training site.

http://www.thesmartmethod.com

Details of all our courses can be found here. Not just Access but also all other Office applications and even an Excel VBA course.

This is a very large site with full course outlines and an on-line quotation and booking system that will instantly quote a price for training at any of our training locations in Europe – or even on-site at your own premises. We also offer training anywhere in the world by special quotation.

Microsoft Consulting coding standards.

http://support.microsoft.com/?kbid=110264

If you want another take on a comprehensive coding standard this is the place to go. Their standard is a superset of the Visual Basic coding conventions found in the Visual Basic "Programmer's Guide". At time of writing version 1.1 last revised on January 9th 2003 was the current version.

The standard is designed for VB6 rather then VBA but almost everything is relevant. We don't disagree with much in this standard but it has nothing that is Access-specific, for example there are no conventions for table and field naming.

The Microsoft Most Valuable Professional site for Access (also called *The Access Web*).

http://www.mvps.org/access

A great site full of comments, hints and code samples specifically for Access.

Hungarian Notation – Charles Simonyi's original paper

http://msdn.microsoft.com/library/default.asp?url=/library/en-us/dnvs600/html/hunganotat.asp

Charles Simonyi's original historic work. Hungarian notation was used as a coding standard inside Microsoft during the development of Microsoft Office. I first adopted some of Symonyi's ideas in 1990 and they massively improved the efficiency of my code. His original paper is a great read and inspired many of our own programming standards.

Index

'
' comment character, 72

&
& concatenation operator, 78

?
? used to print in immediate window, 81

—
_ underscore continuation character, 95

A
access object model, **64**, 132
add record button, of form navigation bar, 128
AddItem, method of combo box object, 61
ADO, 132
AfterUpdate, event of option group control, 142
american english, use of, 13
ApplyFilter, event of form object, 142
argument, 60, 94
    understanding ByRef and ByVal, 98
automatic type conversion, 96

B
beep command, 63
bookmark, property of form object, 123
bookmark, property of recordset object, 123
boolean data type described, 91
bound object frame
    border style property, 213
    size mode property, 35
bound object framesize mode property, 213
breakpoint, 74
bug, defined, 74
build event, shortcut menu option, 73
business rule, adding to a form using VBA, 190
ByRef
    understanding, **98**
ByVal
    understanding, **98**

C
calculated field, in query, 33
call, VBA statement, 73
caption, field property, 21
caption, form property, **96**
caption, label control property, 144
car object model, **64**
cascade delete related record, 29
cascade update related fields, 29
class, terminology explained, 107

cleanup code, use of in error handler, 114
click event, of command button, 73
clip art
    finding suitable clip art on the web (sidebar), 212
    google images, using to find, 242
    inserting into a report, 212
clone, method of recordset object, 123
close, method of DoCmd object, 135
code editor
    build event, access from shortcut menu using, 73
    code button, using to access, 78
    view access button, returning to access with, 74
collection
    about object collections, **58**
    naming in plural of all collections rule, 65
combo box
    AddItem method, 61
    automatic generation of from lookup fields, 34
    automatically selecting an item, 178
    default value, 123
    enabled property, 139
    lookup field, 22
    NewData, parameter of NotInList event, 168
    NotInList event, 168, 196
    recordset property, 190
    requery method, 177
    response, parameter of NotInList event, 168
    self-updating, creating, 168
    set method, 179
    SetFocus method, 179
    synchronising contents with form's current record, 130
    text property, 179
    value property, 131
    wizard generated code, understanding, 116
    wizard, using to create lookup feature, 50
command button
    adding to a form, 48
    cancel property, 158
    click event, 63, 73
    default property, 158
    enabled property, 159
    using to replace navigation bar, 50
    wizard, add new record action, 55, 128
    wizard, close form action, 174
    wizard, delete record action, 48
    wizard, go to first record action, 55
    wizard, go to last record action, 55
    wizard, go to next record action, 55
    wizard, go to previous record action, 55
    wizard, open form action, 160, 174, 176, 243
    wizard, Run MS Word action, 232
    wizard, using, 48
concatenate
    & concatenation operator, 78
    concatenated lookup field, creating, 24
    fields in query designer, 33
constant
    global, creating and using, 172
    vbCrLf, use of, **104**
constrain relationships, 26
continue button on debug toolbar, 93

L

label
  adding control to a form, 144
  caption property, 144
  text align property, 212
late binding, 122, 124, 234
left join, 206
lesson, 14
line, **263**
  shift key, use of to create horizontal and vertical lines, 263
links, **287**
list box
  AfterUpdate event, 159
  browse form, create using, 154
  DblClick event, 159
local scope, 102
locals window (debug tool), 82
long integer data type described, 91
lookup field, 22
  auto conversion to data-driven combo boxes by form wizard, 34
  create a concatenated lookup field, 24
  creating, 22
  lookup tab, 25
  query, designing with understanding of lookup field behavior, 192
  using the lookup wizard, 24

M

many-to-many relationship, 26, 28
many-to-many, subform, implementing, 192
margins
  choosing appropriate sizes (sidebar), 213
  setting for a report, 213
maximize, method of DoCmd object, 135
Me, keyword (sidebar), 101
menu
  bare-bones menu, suggestion for items in, 244
  begin a group, shortcut command, 246
  custom global menu, creating, 244
  custom items, adding to, 248
  custom, creating, **241**
  dividing line, adding to, 246
  forms, adding menu item to open form, 249
  style property of menu items, 250
method
  arguments (parameters), 60
  understanding, 60
minimize, method of DoCmd object, 135
modal, 156
modeless, 156
module level scope, explained, 102
MsgBox
  function described, 73
  passing title argument to, 95
  vbCancel constant, 188
  vbOKCancel constant, 188
  vbQuestion constant, 168, 188
  vbYesNo constant, 168

N

name, form property, **96**
navigation bar

using command buttons to replace, 50, 264
null
  concept of, 31, 143
  in relation to foreign key default values, 31
Nz, VBA function, 123

O

object
  access object model (diagram), 132
  access object model, understanding, 64
  automatic destruction of object variables, discussion, **261**
  class, terminology explained, 107
  collections of, **58**
  CreateObject, VBA function, 234
  destroying, 260
  dot notation, use of, 101
  early binding, 122, 124, 234, 260
  events, understanding, 62
  explicitly declaring, 260
  late binding, 122, 124, 234, 260
  memory leak, avoiding, **261**
  methods, understanding, 60
  object browser, using, 106
  object orientated paradigm explained, **57**
  properties, understanding, **58**
  reference (or pointer) to object, how object variables work, 123
  references, using Tools→References to define, 234
one-to-many relationship, 26
option compare database (sidebar), 93
option explicit, 92
option group, 217
  AfterUpdate event, 142
  enabled property, 143
  null, use of to de-select all options, 143
  tab control, using with, **216**
  using, **140**
  value property, using to establish selected item, 142, 220
  wizard, **140**

P

page break control, adding to a report, 212
parameter, 60, 94
  understanding ByRef and ByVal, 98
parameter-driven query, basing report on, 205
penny rounding problems with floating point data types, 92
Popup form, implementing, 153
popup modal dialog form, 218
precise data type, 91
prefixes for form controls, 126
primary key
  rules, 20
print preview, opening report in, 220
private scope, explained, 102
procedure
  sub procedure, breaking down complex tasks, 72
  understanding, **72**
property
  understanding, **58**
public scope, explained, 102

Q

query. *See Also join*

private, explained, 102
public, explained, 102
understanding, 102
session, 14
first page, 15
session and lesson files, 11
session objectives, 15
SetFocus, method of text box control, 129
shortcut key, adding to a control, 146
show table button, query design toolbar button, 206
size mode, property of bound object frame control, 35
smart method. *See* The Smart Method
sorting and grouping button, report design toolbar, 210
speeding up data entry, **137**
SQL
action query, executing with the DoCmd object's RunSQL method, 169
apostrophes, handling of in SQL queries, 170
asterix (*), use of, 33
equi join, 206
inner join, 206
left join, 206
right join, 206
RunSQL method of DoCmd object, 168, 169
SqlSafe custom function, 171
using SQL queries to underpin wizard-generated forms, 32
Where clause, as used with recordset object's FindFirst method, 123
where clause, using when opening report, 221
startup options
setting, 266
suggested settings, 267
static data, **167**
step into, debug function described, 75
step out, debug function described, **76**
step over, debug function described, **76**
step through code with debug tools, **74**
str prefix, simple explanation, 78
str, VBA function, 123
string data type, **91**
strong typing, **90**, **92**
sub
use of sub and end sub, **72**
sub forms, **187**
subform/subreport wizard, using, 198
switchboard, 241
switchboard manager, 46
wizard, using, 46

T

tab
caption property, 217
using, **216**
tab order, 36
table
field properties, 30
foreign key rules, 21
test
expert beta tester problem (sidebar and discussion), 269
how to, **268**
text box
BackColor property, 149
flat effect, property, 101
locked property, 163
properties described, 100

set and retrieve values from VBA code, 100
SetFocus method, 129
value property, 101
text, property of combo box control, 131
the smart method
informal summary, 15
learning by participation, 17
putting the smart method to work, 14
session objectives, 15
sessions and lessons, 14
two facing pages rule, 16
toggle breakpoint button, on debug toolbar, 74
toolbar
commands, adding to, 244
custom, create, 241, 250
debug toolbar, 74
new, creating, 244
standard commands, adding, 246
toolbox
control wizards button, 48
displaying, 48
tooltip, use to show value of a variable, 81
triggers (sidebar), 191
typographical conventions
american english, use of, 13
summary, 12
tip, important and note sidebars, 16

U

user interface. *See Also menu, toolbar*
custom, creating, **241**
form appearance, improving, **262**
specification, example of, 192
switchboard, 241
switchboard wizard, 46
toolbar, creating custom, **241**

V

validation, **187**
advisory, adding in code, 188
client-side vs server-side, 191
mandatory, adding without code, 188
value, property of combo box control, 131
value, property of text box control, 101
variable
understanding variables, **78**
variant data type described, 91
VBA. *See Also data type, variable, debug, scope, error*
' comment character, 72
& concatenation operator, 78
? (print), 81
_ underscore continuation character, 95
automatic type conversion, 96
beep command, 63
call, use of statement recommended when calling functions and subs, 73
comments, 72
continue button on debug toolbar, 93
CreateObject, function, 234
debug tools, 74
error handling, implementing, **104**
g, use of prefix to denote global level variable, 102
global constant, creating and using, 172
if...then...else...end if construct (sidebar), 139

W

Z

Printed in the United States
210080BV00004B/195-220/A

9 780955 459900